2019 SUPPLEMI

ROTUNDA'S MODERN CONSTITUTIONAL LAW

CASES AND NOTES

Unabridged and Abridged
Eleventh Editions

■ ■ ■

Ronald D. Rotunda
Late Doy & Dee Henley Chair and
Distinguished Professor of Jurisprudence
Dale E. Fowler School of Law
Chapman University

Bennett L. Gershman
Professor of Law, Elisabeth Haub School of Law
Pace University

AMERICAN CASEBOOK SERIES®

WEST
ACADEMIC
PUBLISHING

American Casebook Series is a trademark registered in the U.S. Patent and Trademark Office.

© 2017 LEG, Inc. d/b/a West Academic
© 2019 LEG, Inc. d/b/a West Academic
    444 Cedar Street, Suite 700
    St. Paul, MN 55101
    1-877-888-1330

West, West Academic Publishing, and West Academic are trademarks of West Publishing Corporation, used under license.

Printed in the United States of America

ISBN: 978-1-68467-522-7

To Lissa

PREFACE

Ronald D. Rotunda passed away on March 14, 2018. It is impossible for me to overstate Ron's impact on Constitutional Law and his lasting legacy to those of us who teach Constitutional Law. Ron was a "master" of the subject; indeed, Rotunda is "a major brand name in Constitutional Law."[1] As one obituary observed, "It is difficult to believe this brilliant dynamo of legal scholarship, wonderful erudition, and wily wit is gone."[2]

The first edition of Ron's classic, *Modern Constitutional Law*, was published in 1980, and his last edition—the 11th (both unabridged and abridged versions)—35 years later.[3] Ron's last addition to his casebook is contained in this Supplement and covers the Court's 2014–2016 terms. The Court's newest member at that time—Neil M. Gorsuch—took the bench on April 10, 2017. Since then, Justice Anthony Kennedy retired and President Donald Trump nominated Brett Kavanaugh, who was confirmed by the Senate on October 6, 2018 (50 Senators in favor; 48 opposed). He assumed the bench October 8, 2018.

This Supplement covers the 2014–2018 terms which cover a wide field of Constitutional Law. In three cases the Court overruled longstanding precedents. In *Franchise Tax Board of California v. Hyatt*, 139 S.Ct. 1485 (2019), the Court overruled *Nevada v. Hall*, 440 U.S. 410 (1979), and held that states have sovereign immunity in lawsuits in other states. In *South Dakota v. Wayfair*, 138 S.Ct. 2080 (2018), the Court overruled *Quill Corp. v. North Dakota*, 504 U.S. 298 (1992) and *National Bellas Hess, Inc. v. Department of Revenue of Ill.*, 386 U.S. 753 (1976), and held that an out-of-state company's physical presence in the taxing state is not necessary for that state to require the seller to collect and remit its sales tax. In *Janus v. American Federation of State, County, and Municipal Employees, Council 31*, 138 S.Ct. 2448 (2018), the Court overruled *Abood v. Detroit Bd. of Ed.*, 431 U.S. 209 (1977), and held that the right of public employees to freedom of speech is violated if they are compelled to pay dues to a union about whose positions they object.

---

[1] Thomas E. Baker, *Mastering Modern Constitutional Law,* 21 SEATTLE U. L. REV. 927, 929 (1998).

[2] John Dean, *R.I.P. Ron Rotunda—A Man Responsible for Watergate's Most Lasting Positive Impact,* VERDICT (March 14, 2018).

[3] In addition to his casebook, Ron has coauthored a leading hornbook on the subject, and a multi-volume treatise. See Ronald D. Rotunda & John E. Nowak, *Treatise on Constitutional Law: Substance and Procedure* (5th ed., Westlaw Thomson Reuters 2012–2013)(with annual pocket parts)(6 volumes). See also, John E. Nowak & Ronald D. Rotunda, *Constitutional Law* (West Pub., West Hornbook Series, 8th ed. 2010), and Ronald D. Rotunda & John E. Nowak, *Principles of Constitutional Law* (West Academic, Concise Hornbook Series, 5th ed. 2016).

During the 2014 term the Court (5–4) held that there is a constitutional right to same-sex marriage under the Due Process and Equal Protection Clauses, *Obergefell v. Hodges,* 135 S.Ct. 2584 (2015). During the 2015 term the Court (5–3) struck down a Texas statute (6–3) that required abortion providers to have admitting privileges at a local hospital and also required abortion facilities to meet minimum standards for ambulatory surgical centers. The Court held that these regulations imposed an undue burden on a woman's right to obtain an abortion. This was the first case since 1992 that Justice Kennedy joined to invalidate a law regulating abortion as an "undue burden."

The Court decided four cases involving religious freedom, religious tolerance, and government hostility to religion. In *Trump v. Hawaii,* 138 S.Ct. 2392 (2018), the Court (5–4) held that President Trump's Proclamation barring entry into the United States of nationals from seven countries, five of which have Muslim-majority populations, was well within the President's foreign policy powers to protect national security and under rational basis review was not shown to be based on religious animus. In *American Legion v. American Humanist Assn.,* 139 S.Ct. 2067 (2019), the Court upheld the maintenance of a large Cross at a busy public intersection that had been at the site for over ninety years and that may have acquired historical rather than religious symbolism; it therefore did not violate the Establishment Clause, and, in fact, removing it might actually suggest an aggressive hostility to religion. In *Masterpiece Cakeshop, Ltd. v. Colorado Civil Rights Commission,* 138 S.Ct. 1719 (2018), the Court sidestepped the "difficult question" of reconciling the rights and dignity of gay persons who wish to be married but who face discrimination when they seek goods or services, finding instead that the Colorado Civil Rights Commission did not give neutral and respectful consideration to a baker's claim that creating the cake would violate his religious beliefs. Finally, in *Trinity Lutheran Church of Columbia, Inc. v. Comer,* 137 S.Ct. 2012 (2017), the Court (6–2) invalidated a Missouri program that offered state grants to public and private schools to purchase rubber playground surfaces but disqualified churches from receiving grants. The Court held that the program imposed an unconstitutional penalty on the free exercise of religion.

In two freedom of speech cases the Court reinforced its approach to government-compelled speech. In *National Institute of Life Advocates v. Becerra,* 138 S.Ct. 2361 (2018), the Court (5–4) struck down a California regulation that required pro-life crisis-pregnancy centers to notify women that California provides free or low-cost services, including abortions, holding that the notice requirement compelled petitioners to deliver a particular message—the very practice that petitioners opposed—thereby violating their First Amendment right to free speech. And in *Janus,* noted above, the Court (5–4) struck down the union fee requirement for public employees, holding that it likewise compelled persons to speak on subjects of which they disapproved. After holding that certain kinds of speech can be excluded from inside and outside polling places, [see *Burson v. Freeman*, 504 U.S. 191 (1992)(upholding a Tennessee law prohibiting solicitation of votes and display of campaign materials within 100 feet of polling place)], the Court in *Minnesota Voters Alliance v. Mansky*, 138 S.Ct. 1876 (2018) struck down a state law prohibiting individuals from wearing political badges or attire inside a polling place as too indefinite since the term "political" is subject to "haphazard and indeterminate interpretations." After previously finding that certain language in the Lanham Act banning trademarks that disparage people violated the right to free speech, see *Matal v. Tam*, 137 S.Ct. 1744 (2017), the Court in *Iancu v. Brunetti*, 139 S.Ct. 2292 (2019) struck down under the First Amendment a neighboring provision barring marks that are "immoral" or "scandalous."

In two other free speech cases, the Court unanimously struck down a local sign ordinance as a content-based regulation of speech, *Reed v. Town of Gilbert*, 135 S.Ct. 2218 (2015) and upheld (5–4) the refusal of Texas under its speciality license plate program to issue a plate to an applicant that featured a Confederate battle flag design, holding that the Texas program constitutes government speech.

The Court decided two cases under the Commerce Clause. In *Murphy v. National Collegiate Athletic Association*, 138 S.Ct. 1461 (2018), the Court amplified the "anti-commandeering" doctrine of *New York v. United States*, 505 U.S. 144 (1992) and *Printz v. United States*, 521 U.S. 898 (1997), striking down the Professional and Amateur Sports Protection Act, which the Court held unconstitutionally infringed on the sovereign authority of States to regulate sports gambling by preventing States from repealing laws prohibiting sports gambling or enacting laws authorizing sports gambling. And in *Tennessee Wine and Spirits Retailers Assn. v. Russell F. Thomas, Executive Director of the Tennessee Alcohol Beverage Commission*, 139 S.Ct. 2449 (2019), the Court amplified its ruling in *Granholm v. Heald*, 544 U.S. 460 (2005), that the 21st Amendment does not authorize states to discriminate in the regulation of alcohol.

Two significant cases were decided on the last day of the Court's 2018 term. Both decision were 5–4, both reflected the current Court's new dynamics and uncertain coalitions, and both were authored by Chief Justice Roberts for different four-Justice pluralities. In *Rucho v. Common Cause*, 139 S.Ct. 2484 (2019), the Court (Roberts, C.J., joined by Thomas, Alito, Gorsuch, & Kavanaugh, JJ.) after years of indecision as to whether partisan gerrymandering presented a justiciable question, decided that it did not; there are no clear, manageable, and politically neutral standards to correct district lines that were drawn for partisan reasons and therefore federal courts have no business adjudicating what is essentially a "political question." And in *Department of Commerce v. New York*, 139 S.Ct. 2551 (2019), the Court (Roberts, C.J., joined by Ginsburg, Breyer, Sotomayor, & Kagan, JJ.) affirmed a lower court order striking down the citizenship question on the federal census, finding that the reasons given by the Trump administration for including that question were "contrived" and therefore arbitrary and capricious under the Administrative Procedure Act.

As the Court prepares for the 2019 term and beyond, there are significant questions regarding the continued development of Constitutional Law. One cannot ignore the comment made by Justice Breyer in his dissent in *Franchise Tax Board*, noted above, overruling *Nevada v. Hall*: "Today's decision can only cause one to wonder which cases the Court will overrule next." One potential candidate may be the Court's venerable "Non-Delegation" doctrine which in *United States v. Gundy*, 139 S.Ct. 2116 (2019) was reaffirmed by a plurality in upholding the Sex Offender Registration and Notification Act (SORNA). Justice Alito agreed that the statute contains an adequate standard and should be upheld under the traditional approach the Court has taken, but observed that if "a majority of the Court were willing to reconsider the approach we have taken for 84 years, I would support that effort." With four Justices dissenting in *Gundy*, the non-delegation doctrine appears ripe for overruling.

Also vulnerable is *Lemon v. Kurtzman*, 403 U.S. 602 (1971), which the Court has applied off and on for nearly fifty years in reviewing Establishment Clause cases. Given that four Justices in the *American Legion* decision involving the public display of the Cross indicated their dissatisfaction with the *Lemon* test, that case too may be ripe for overruling. Finally, the Court will almost certainly revisit the constitutional conflict that was presented in *Masterpiece Cakeshop* between protecting the religious freedom of a vendor of goods and services and the right of individuals from discrimination. And, of course, there is *Roe v. Wade*.

I am grateful to several people for helping me preserve and perpetuate Ronald Rotunda's legacy. Professor Thomas E. Baker, eminent constitutional scholar and founding member of the Florida International University College of Law, generously shared his essential insights and advice; Professor Donald Doernberg, my former colleague and brilliant scholar of the federal courts, offered critical comments and suggestions; Professors Emily Waldman and Lissa Griffin, my colleagues, have given encouragement and advice; and Vicky Gannon, always there for research, technical, and logistical support. I am also thankful to the many people at West Academic who have made this supplement possible, especially Louis Higgins, Sarah Bowser Agan, and Greg Olson.

Here are Ron's final words from the Preface to the 11th Edition:

Bismarck said that laws are like sausages—one should not see how they are made. As tastes change and less filler is added to the making of sausage, some people fear that more is being added to the making of laws. Well, I have seen sausage being made (for two summers, while working the graveyard shift at a meat packing plant), and I have seen the Court make law. It is not like making sausage. Instead, our state and federal courts have protected our system of Constitutional liberties and made us the envy of the world. When we talk of imports and exports, we usually think of such things as farm goods, automobiles, and intellectual property. However, our greatest export is our Bill of Rights, which is why, when people around the world seek to preserve freedom, they often seek to emulate our judicial system.

BENNETT L. GERSHMAN

White Plains, New York
July, 2019

Summary of Contents

TABLE OF CONTENTS

TABLE OF CASES

The principal cases are in bold type.

January 2019. Seated, from the left: Associate Justice Stephen Breyer, Associate Justice Clarence Thomas, Chief Justice John Roberts, Associate Justice Ruth Bader Ginsburg, Associate Justice Samuel Alito Jr. Standing, from left: Associate Justice Neil Gorsuch, Associate Justice Sonia Sotomayor, Associate Justice Elena Kagan, Associate Justice Brett Kavanaugh.

2019 SUPPLEMENT TO

ROTUNDA'S MODERN CONSTITUTIONAL LAW

CASES AND NOTES

Unabridged and Abridged
Eleventh Editions

CHAPTER 1

JUDICIAL REVIEW

■ ■ ■

1–2 LIMITATIONS ON THE EXERCISE OF JUDICIAL REVIEW

1–2.2 STATUTORY RESTRICTIONS

Unabridged, p. 41; add to end of *Notes*, new Note 5:

Abridged, p. 40; add to end of *Notes*, new Note 5:

5. FACILITATING CAUSES OF ACTION. *Bank Markazi v. Peterson,* 578 U.S. ____, 136 S.Ct. 1310, 194 L.Ed.2d 463 (2016). Bank Markazi is the Central Bank of Iran. Respondents included more than 1,000 victims of Iran-sponsored acts of terrorism, their estate representatives, and surviving family members. They sued Iran for terrorist acts. To enforce judgments they obtained by default, they moved for turnover of about $1.75 billion in bond assets held in a New York bank account. Respondents alleged that Bank Markazi, the Central Bank of Iran owned these assets.

When Respondents learned of bonds in a New York bank that the U.S. Government had frozen, they went after them. The turnover began in 2008. In 2012, Congress enacted the Iran Threat Reduction and Syria Human Rights Act of 2012. 22 U.S.C. § 8772. That statute makes a designated set of assets available to satisfy the judgments underlying a consolidated enforcement proceeding, which the statute specifically identifies by the District Court's docket number. Section 8772(a)(2) requires a court to determine, before allowing execution against these assets, "whether Iran holds equitable title to, or the beneficial interest in, the assets." Justice Ginsburg, for the Court, held that § 8772, is constitutional.

Bank Markazi argued that § 8772 violates separation of powers by purporting to change the law and direct a particular result in a single pending case. Ginsburg admitted that § 8772 "is an unusual statute: It designates a particular set of assets and renders them available to satisfy the liability and damages judgments underlying a consolidated enforcement proceeding that the statute identifies by the District Court's docket number." However, this law simply facilitates execution of judgments in 16 suits. While Congress may not force the courts to reopen final judgments, it has the power to make valid statutes retroactively applicable to pending cases. Moreover,

§ 8772 is an exercise of congressional authority regarding foreign affairs, where the controlling role of the political bodies is both necessary and proper.

Roberts, C.J., dissenting (joined by Sotomayor, J.) acknowledged, "the rule that courts generally must apply a retroactively applicable statute to pending cases." Still, he argued, this law violates separation of powers because "Congress has decided this case by enacting a bespoke statute tailored to this case that resolves the parties' specific legal disputes to guarantee respondents victory."

1–2.3 ADVISORY OPINIONS

Unabridged, p. 49; add to end of *Notes*, new Note 9:

Abridged, p. 49; add to end of *Notes*, new Note 9:

9. INTERSTATE SOVEREIGN IMMUNITY. *Franchise Tax Board of California v. Hyatt,* 139 S.Ct. 1485, ___ L.Ed.2d ___ (2019). *Nevada v. Hall,* 440 U.S. 410 (1979) held that the Constitution does not bar private suits against a state in the courts of another state and that under principles of comity, states as sovereigns could grant or deny immunity to the other state. The Court, in an opinion by Thomas, J. (5–4), overruled *Hall*. According to the majority, *Hall* misreads the historical record, is inconsistent with the Court's sovereign immunity jurisprudence, and is irreconcilable with the Constitution's structure. California's Franchise Tax Board was sued by Gilbert Hyatt in a Nevada state court for torts he alleged the Board committed in conducting an eleven-year audit of his taxes. The Nevada court rejected California's argument that it was entitled to immunity, holding that under principles of comity the California Board was entitled to the same immunity that Nevada law afforded Nevada agencies—immunity from negligent but not intentional torts. *Hall* inferred that since the Constitution did not expressly grant sovereign immunity to the states, the states under the Tenth Amendment retained the power in their own courts to deny immunity to other states. That inference, according to the majority, is incorrect. The Constitution's design "fundamentally adjusts the States' relationship with each other and curtails their ability, as sovereigns, to decline to recognize each other's immunity." The Court sketched the historical context and the immunity principles of the common law and international law which "took as given that States could not be haled involuntarily before each other's courts." The Court's early "blunder" in *Chisolm v. Georgia,* 2 Dall. 419 (1793), which allowed private suits in state courts, led to the swift passage of the Eleventh Amendment, "which confirmed that the Constitution was not meant to 'raise up' any suits against the States that were 'anomalous and unheard of when the Constitution was adopted,'" [quoting *Hans v. Louisiana,* 134 U.S. 1, 18 (1890)]. Interstate sovereign immunity is "integral" to the structure of the Constitution and "implicit" as an essential component of federalism."

Breyer, J., joined by Ginsburg, Sotomayor, & Kagan, JJ., dissented, arguing that there is no good reason to overrule *Hall*. Under *Hall,* the Constitution took a permissive approach, leaving it up to each state to decide whether to grant or deny its sister states sovereign immunity. Indeed, as *Hall* observed, "compelling states to grant immunity to their sister states would risk interfering with sovereign rights that the Tenth Amendment leaves to the states." The Constitution does not expressly afford states absolute immunity, and there is nothing "implicit," "embedded in," or "within the constitutional design," as the majority insists, that confers this power. *Hall* "is a well-reasoned decision that has caused no serious practical problems." But even if *Hall* was wrongly decided, that "cannot by itself justify scrapping settled precedent." The few cases since *Hall* in which one state entertained a private citizen's suit against another state (14 cases in 40 years) shows that "most states, like most sovereign nations, are reluctant to deny a sister state the immunity that they would prefer to enjoy reciprocally." It is one thing to overrule a settled precedent when the rule "defies practical workability" or facts have changed to "rob the old rule of significant application or justification." However, "it is far more dangerous to overrule a decision only because five Members of a later Court come to agree with earlier dissenters on a difficult legal question." The dissenters concluded: "Today's decision can only cause one to wonder which cases the Court will overrule next."

1–2.4 POLITICAL QUESTIONS

Unabridged, p. 67; add to end of *Notes*:

Abridged, p. 63; add to end of *Notes*:

In *Gill v. Whitford*, 138 S.Ct. 1916, 201 L.Ed.2d 313 (2018), twelve Democratic voters challenged Wisconsin's 2010 districting plan (Act 43) as unconstitutionally diluting the ability of the Democratic Party to convert Democratic votes into Democratic seats in the single-member legislative districts. The plaintiffs alleged that the legislative plan accomplished this by "cracking" Democratic voters in multiple districts so that the candidates would typically fall short of a majority in each one of these districts, and "packing" other Democratic voters into a few districts in which Democratic candidates always win by overwhelming margins. The plaintiffs sought to show the extent to which cracking and packing favored one political party by a so-called "efficiency gap" which compared each party's "wasted" votes—votes cast for a losing candidate or a winning candidate in excess of what that candidate needs to win—across all legislative districts. The plaintiffs argued that enforcement of Act 43 would violate their First Amendment right of association and their Fourteenth Amendment right to equal protection. They alleged that regardless of whether they themselves resided in a district that was packed or cracked, they were harmed by the manipulation of district boundaries because Democrats statewide do not have the same opportunity provided to Republicans to elect representatives of their choice.

The defendants moved to dismiss the claims, arguing that the plaintiffs lacked standing to challenge the constitutionality of Act 43 because as individual voters their legally protected interests existed only with respect to the makeup of the legislative districts in which they resided and voted. The three-judge District Court denied the motion and following a trial concluded that Act 43 was an unconstitutional partisan gerrymander. The court held that the plaintiffs had standing because they suffered a particularized injury to their equal protection rights.

The Supreme Court, in an opinion by Chief Justice Roberts, vacated the District Court's order as to standing, holding that the plaintiffs failed to demonstrate a particularized injury sufficient to support Article III standing. The Court remanded the case so the plaintiffs would have an opportunity to show a concrete and particularized injury. The Court observed that its previous attempts to decide what judicially enforceable limits, if any, the Constitution sets on partisan gerrymandering "have left few clear landmarks" and "have generated conflicting views both of how to conceive of the injury arising from partisan gerrymandering and of the appropriate role for the Federal Judiciary in remedying that injury." Past cases have noted that political considerations in districting "inevitably has and is intended to have substantial political consequences," *Gaffney v. Cummings;* that challengers would have to "prove both intentional discrimination against an identifiable political group and an actual discriminatory effect on that group," *Davis v. Bandemer* (plurality); that partisan gerrymandering claims "were nonjusticiable because there was no judicially discernible and manageable standard by which to decide them," *Vieth v. Jubelirer* (plurality); and that proving partisan bias "sheds[s] no light on how much partisan dominance is too much" and "asymmetry alone is not a reliable measure of unconstitutional partisanship," *League of United Latin American Citizens v. Perry (LULAC).*

The Court's efforts in the above cases leave "unresolved" two threshold questions: first, what is necessary to show standing, and second, whether the claims are justiciable. The Court deferred on the second question because the plaintiffs did not show they had standing. Since a person's right to vote is "personal and individual," a plaintiff to get standing must allege facts showing that he resided in a district in which his vote was "wasted" by packing or cracking, and that the proper remedy for that violation is to revise the boundaries of that individual's district. "A plaintiff who complains of gerrymandering, but who does not live in a gerrymandered district, asserts only a generalized grievance against governmental conduct of which he or she does not approve." However, the plaintiffs' claim that their legal injury is not limited to the injury they have suffered as individual voters but extends to statewide harm to their collective interest in being fairly represented in the overall composition of the legislature has not yet been found by the Court to present an individual and personal injury of the kind required for Article III standing. The "fundamental problem with the plaintiffs' case" is that it presents a case of "group political interests, not individual legal rights." "This Court is not responsible for vindicating generalized partisan preferences. The

Court's constitutionally prescribed role is to vindicate the individual rights of the people appearing before it." Since this case involves an unsettled claim with unresolved questions of justiciability, the Court remanded the case to allow the plaintiffs to prove concrete and particularized injuries with evidence tending to show a burden on their individual votes.

Justice Kagan, joined by Ginsburg, Breyer, & Sotomayor, JJ., agreed with the Court's conclusions but wrote separately to address the kind of evidence the plaintiffs must offer to support their allegations. To show that his or her vote was diluted by packing or cracking, a plaintiff could produce an alternative map or maps which was drawn consistent with traditional districting principles and without a focus on partisan advantage. To prove the mapmaker's illicit partisan intent, a plaintiff could show that the mapmaker consulted partisan voting data and graded draft maps according to the amount of advantage those maps conferred on Republicans. To be sure, remedying each plaintiff's vote dilution injury requires revising only those districts in which a plaintiff resides, but with enough plaintiffs joined together, "attacking all the packed and cracked districts in a statewide gerrymander could amount to a wholesale restructuring of the State's districting plan."

In addition to showing how partisan gerrymandering dilutes individual votes, the dissenters also argued that partisan gerrymandering infringes the First Amendment right of association which is distinct from vote dilution and would entail a different standing inquiry. The harm alleged here results from the State purposely subjecting a group of voters or their party to disfavored treatment which burdens the group's representational rights and natural political strength to fundraise, register voters, attract volunteers, and recruit candidates to run for office. Even though a voter's district has been left untouched by a partisan gerrymander, "if the gerrymander ravaged the party he works to support, then he indeed suffers harm, as do all other involved members of that party." Thus, "when the harm alleged is not district specific, the proof needed for standing should not be district specific either." In this case, the plaintiffs did not sufficiently advance an associational theory. But nothing in the Court's opinion prevents the plaintiffs on remand from pursuing an associational claim.

RUCHO, ET AL. V. COMMON CAUSE, ET AL.

139 S.Ct. 2484, ___ L.Ed.2d ___ (2019).

CHIEF JUSTICE ROBERTS delivered the opinion of the Court.

Voters and other plaintiffs in North Carolina and Maryland challenged their States' congressional districting maps as unconstitutional partisan gerrymanders. The North Carolina plaintiffs complained that the State's districting plan discriminated against Democrats; the Maryland plaintiffs complained that their State's plan discriminated against Republicans. . . . The districting plans at issue here are highly partisan, by any measure. The question is whether the courts below appropriately exercised judicial power when they found them unconstitutional as well.

The first case involves a challenge to the congressional redistricting plan enacted by the Republican-controlled North Carolina General Assembly in 2016. The Republican legislators leading the redistricting effort instructed their mapmaker to use political data to draw a map that would produce a congressional delegation of ten Republicans and three Democrats. As one of the two Republicans chairing the redistricting committee stated, "I think electing Republicans is better than electing Democrats. So I drew this map to help foster what I think is better for the country.". . . [In the second case], in 2011, the Maryland Legislature—dominated by Democrats—undertook to redraw the lines of that State's eight congressional districts. The Governor at the time, Democrat Martin O'Malley, led the process. The Governor later testified that his aim was to "use the redistricting process to change the overall composition of Maryland's congressional delegation to 7 Democrats and 1 Republican by flipping" one district. The 2011 Plan accomplished that by moving roughly 360,000 voters out of the Sixth District and moving 350,000 new voters in. Overall, the Plan reduced the number of registered Republicans in the Sixth District by about 66,000 and increased the number of registered Democrats by about 24,000. . . .

Article III of the Constitution limits federal courts to deciding "Cases" and "Controversies." We have understood that limitation to mean that federal courts can address only questions "historically viewed as capable of resolution through the judicial process." *Flast v. Cohen.* . . . The question here is whether there is an "appropriate role for the Federal Judiciary" in remedying the problem of partisan gerrymandering—whether such claims are claims of legal right, resolvable according to legal principles, or political questions that must find their resolution elsewhere.

Partisan gerrymandering is nothing new. Nor is frustration with it. The practice was known in the Colonies prior to Independence, and the Framers were familiar with it at the time of the drafting and ratification of the Constitution. . . . The Framers addressed the election of Representatives to Congress in the Elections Clause. Art. I, § 4, cl. 1. That provision assigns to state legislatures the power to prescribe the "Times, Places and Manner of holding Elections" for Members of Congress, while giving Congress the power to "make or alter" any such regulations. . . . Congress has regularly exercised its Elections Clause power, including to address partisan gerrymandering. . . . Starting in the 1950s, Congress enacted a series of laws to protect the right to vote through measures such as the suspension of literacy tests and the prohibition of English-only elections.

Appellants suggest that, through the Elections Clause, the Framers set aside electoral issues such as the one before us as questions that only Congress can resolve. We do not agree. In two areas—one-person, one-vote and racial gerrymandering—our cases have held that there is a role for the courts with respect to at least some issues that could arise from a State's drawing of congressional districts. See *Wesberry v. Sanders*; *Shaw v. Reno.* . . . But the history is not irrelevant. The Framers were aware of electoral districting problems and considered what to do about them. They settled on a characteristic approach, assigning the issue to the state legislatures, expressly checked and balanced by the Federal Congress. At no point was there a suggestion that the federal courts had a role to play. Nor was there any indication that the Framers had ever heard of courts doing such a thing . . . Partisan gerrymandering claims have proved far more difficult to adjudicate. The basic reason is that, while it is illegal for a jurisdiction to depart from the one-person, one-vote rule, or to engage in racial discrimination in districting, "a jurisdiction may engage in constitutional political gerrymandering." *Hunt v. Cromartie,* 526 U.S. 541, 551 (1999). . . To hold that legislators cannot take partisan interests into account when drawing district lines would essentially countermand the Framers' decision to entrust districting to political entities. The "central problem" is not determining whether a jurisdiction has engaged in partisan gerrymandering. It is "determining when political gerrymandering has gone too far." *Vieth.*

In considering whether partisan gerrymandering claims are justiciable, we are mindful of Justice Kennedy's counsel in *Vieth:* Any standard for resolving such claims must be grounded in a "limited and precise rationale" and be "clear, manageable, and politically neutral." An expansive standard requiring "the correction of all election district lines drawn for partisan reasons would commit federal and state courts to unprecedented intervention in the American political process," *Vieth.*

Partisan gerrymandering claims rest on an instinct that groups with a certain level of political support should enjoy a commensurate level of political power and influence. Partisan gerrymandering claims invariably sound in a desire for proportional representation. Our cases, however, clearly foreclose any claim that the Constitution requires proportional representation or that legislatures in reapportioning must draw district lines to come as near as possible to allocating seats to the contending parties in proportion to what their anticipated statewide vote will be. The Founders certainly did not think proportional representation was required. For more than 50 years after ratification of the Constitution, many States elected their congressional representatives through at-large or "general ticket" elections. Such States typically sent single-party delegations to Congress. . . .

Unable to claim that the Constitution requires proportional representation outright, plaintiffs inevitably ask the courts to make their own political judgment about how much representation particular political parties deserve—based on the votes of their supporters—and to rearrange the challenged districts to achieve that end. But federal courts are not equipped to apportion political power as a matter of fairness, nor is there any basis for concluding that they were authorized to do so. The initial difficulty in settling on a "clear, manageable and politically neutral" test for fairness is that it is not even clear what fairness looks like in this context. There is a large measure of "unfairness" in any winner-take-all system. Fairness may mean a greater number of competitive districts. Such a claim seeks to undo packing and cracking so that supporters of the disadvantaged party have a better shot at electing their preferred candidates. But making as many districts as possible more competitive could be a recipe for disaster for the disadvantaged party. . .

On the other hand, perhaps the ultimate objective of a "fairer" share of seats in the congressional delegation is most readily achieved by yielding to the gravitational pull of proportionality and engaging in cracking and packing, to ensure each party its "appropriate" share of "safe" seats. Such an approach, however, comes at the expense of competitive districts and of individuals in districts allocated to the opposing party. Or perhaps fairness should be measured by adherence to "traditional" districting criteria, such as maintaining political subdivisions, keeping communities of interest together, and protecting incumbents. . .

Deciding among just these different visions of fairness (you can imagine many others) poses basic questions that are political, not legal. There are no legal standards discernible in the Constitution for making such judgments, let alone limited and precise standards that are clear, manageable, and politically neutral. Any judicial decision on what is "fair" in this context would be an "unmoored determination" of the sort characteristic of a political question beyond the competence of the federal courts. And it is only after determining how to define fairness that you can even begin to answer the determinative question: "How much is too much?" At what point does permissible partisanship become unconstitutional? If compliance with traditional districting criteria is the fairness touchstone, for example, how much deviation from those criteria is constitutionally acceptable and how should mapdrawers prioritize competing criteria?. . .

If a court instead focused on the respective number of seats in the legislature, it would have to decide the ideal number of seats for each party and determine at what point deviation from that balance went too far. If a 5–3 allocation corresponds most closely to statewide vote totals, is a 6–2 allocation permissible, given that legislatures have the authority to engage in a certain degree of partisan gerrymandering? Which seats should be packed and which cracked? Or if the goal is as many competitive districts as possible, how close does the split need to be for the district to be considered competitive? Presumably not all districts could qualify, so how to choose? Even assuming the court knew which version of fairness to be looking for, there are no discernible and manageable standards for deciding whether there has been a violation. The questions are "unguided and ill suited to the development of judicial standards." *Vieth.*

Appellees contend that if we can adjudicate one-person, one-vote claims, we can also assess partisan gerrymandering claims. But the one-person, one-vote rule is relatively easy to administer as a matter of math. The same cannot be said of partisan gerrymandering claims, because the Constitution supplies no objective measure for assessing whether a districting map treats a political party fairly. It hardly follows from the principle that each person must have an equal say in the election of representatives that a person is entitled to have his political party achieve representation in some way commensurate to its share of statewide support.

More fundamentally, "vote dilution" in the one-person, one-vote cases refers to the idea that each vote must carry equal weight. In other words, each representative must be accountable to (approximately) the same number of constituents. That requirement does not extend to political parties. It does not mean that each party must be influential in proportion to its number of supporters. As we stated unanimously in *Gill,* "this Court is not responsible for vindicating generalized partisan preferences. The Court's constitutionally prescribed role is to vindicate the individual rights of the people appearing before it."

Nor do our racial gerrymandering cases provide an appropriate standard for assessing partisan gerrymandering. . . . Unlike partisan gerrymandering claims, a racial gerrymandering claim does not ask for a fair share of political power and influence, with all the justiciability conundrums that entails. It asks instead for the elimination of a racial classification. A partisan gerrymandering claim cannot ask for the elimination of partisanship.

Appellees and the dissent propose a number of "tests" for evaluating partisan gerrymandering claims, but none meets the need for a limited and precise standard that is judicially discernible and manageable. . . . The District Court's "predominant intent" prong is borrowed from the racial gerrymandering context. In racial gerrymandering cases, we rely on a "predominant intent" inquiry to determine whether race was, in fact, the reason particular district boundaries were drawn the way they were. But determining that lines were drawn on the basis of partisanship does not indicate that the districting was improper. A permissible intent—securing partisan advantage—does not become constitutionally impermissible, like racial discrimination, when that permissible intent "predominates." The District Court tried to limit the reach of its test by requiring plaintiffs to show, in addition to predominant partisan intent, that vote dilution "is likely to persist" to such a degree that the elected representative will feel free to ignore the concerns of the supporters of the minority party. But "[t]o allow district courts to strike down apportionment plans on the basis of their prognostications as to the outcome of future elections . . . invites 'findings' on matters as to which neither judges nor anyone else can have any confidence." *Bandemer.* . . .

The appellees assure us that "the persistence of a party's advantage may be shown through sensitivity testing: probing how a plan would perform under other plausible electoral conditions.". . . Even the most sophisticated districting maps cannot reliably account for some of the reasons voters prefer one candidate over another, or why their preferences may change. It is hard to see what the District Court's third prong—providing the defendant an opportunity to show that the discriminatory effects were due to a "legitimate redistricting objective"—adds to the inquiry. The first prong already requires the plaintiff to prove that partisan advantage predominates. Asking whether a legitimate purpose other than partisanship was the motivation for a particular districting map just restates the question.

The District Courts also found partisan gerrymandering claims justiciable under the First Amendment, coalescing around a basic three-part test: proof of intent to burden individuals based on their voting history or party affiliation; an actual burden on political speech or associational rights; and a causal link between the invidious intent and actual burden. . . .

To begin, there are no restrictions on speech, association, or any other First Amendment activities in the districting plans at issue. The plaintiffs are free to engage in those activities no matter what the effect of a plan may be on their district. The plaintiffs' argument is that partisanship in districting should be regarded as simple discrimination against supporters of the opposing party on the basis of political viewpoint. Under that theory, any level of partisanship in districting would constitute an infringement of their First Amendment rights. . . As for actual burden, the slight anecdotal evidence found sufficient by the District Courts in these cases shows that this too is not a serious standard for separating constitutional from unconstitutional partisan gerrymandering. The District Courts relied on testimony about difficulty drumming up volunteers and enthusiasm. How much of a decline in voter engagement is enough to constitute a First Amendment burden? How many door knocks must go unanswered? How many petitions unsigned? How many calls for volunteers unheeded?. . . .

The dissent proposes using a State's own districting criteria as a neutral baseline from which to measure how extreme a partisan gerrymander is. The dissent would have us line up all the possible maps drawn using those criteria according to the partisan distribution they would produce. Distance from the "median" map would indicate whether a particular districting plan harms supporters of one party to an unconstitutional extent. As an initial matter, it does not make sense to use criteria that will vary from State to State and year to year as the baseline for determining whether a gerrymander violates the Federal Constitution. The degree of partisan advantage that the Constitution tolerates should not turn on criteria offered by the gerrymanderers themselves. . . . Even if we were to accept the dissent's proposed baseline, it would return us to the original unanswerable question (How much political motivation and effect is too much?).

The dissent argues that there are other instances in law where matters of degree are left to the courts. For example, the dissent cites the need to determine "substantial anticompetitive effect[s]" in antitrust law. Common experience gives content to terms such as "substantial risk" or "substantial harm," but the same cannot be said of substantial deviation from a median map. There is no way to tell whether the prohibited deviation from that map should kick in at 25 percent or 75 percent or some other point. The only provision in the Constitution that specifically addresses the matter assigns it to the political branches.

The North Carolina District Court further concluded that the 2016 Plan violated the Elections Clause and Article I, § 2. We are unconvinced by that novel approach. The plurality in *Vieth* concluded—without objection from any other Justice—that neither § 2 nor § 4 of Article I "provides a judicially enforceable limit on the political considerations that the States and Congress may take into account when districting. The District Court nevertheless asserted that partisan gerrymanders violate "the core principle of [our] republican government" preserved in Art. I, § 2, "namely, that the voters should choose their representatives, not the other way around." That seems like an objection more properly grounded in the Guarantee Clause of Article IV, § 4, which "guarantee[s] to every State in [the] Union a Republican Form of Government." This Court has several times concluded, however, that the Guarantee Clause does not provide the basis for a justiciable claim.

Excessive partisanship in districting leads to results that reasonably seem unjust. But the fact that such gerrymandering is "incompatible with democratic principles," *Arizona State Legislature,* does not mean that the solution lies with the federal judiciary. We conclude that partisan gerrymandering claims present political questions beyond the reach of the federal courts. Federal judges have no license to reallocate political power between the two major political parties, with no plausible grant of authority in the Constitution, and no legal standards to limit and direct their decisions. "[J]udicial action must be governed by standard, by rule," and must be "principled, rational, and based upon reasoned distinctions" found in the Constitution or laws. *Vieth*. Judicial review of partisan gerrymandering does not meet those basic requirements. . . .

What the appellees and dissent seek is an unprecedented expansion of judicial power. We have never struck down a partisan gerrymander as unconstitutional—despite various requests over the past 45 years. The expansion of judicial authority would not be into just any area of controversy, but into one of the most intensely partisan aspects of American political life. That intervention would be unlimited in scope and duration—it would recur over and over again around the country with each new round of districting, for state as well as federal representatives. Consideration of the impact of today's ruling on democratic principles cannot ignore the effect of the unelected and politically unaccountable branch of the Federal Government assuming such an extraordinary and unprecedented role.

Our conclusion does not condone excessive partisan gerrymandering. Nor does our conclusion condemn complaints about districting to echo into a void. The States, for example, are actively addressing the issue on a number of fronts. In 2015, the Supreme Court of Florida struck down that State's congressional districting plan as a violation of the Fair Districts Amendment to the Florida Constitution. Provisions in state statutes and state constitutions can provide standards and guidance for state courts to apply. Indeed, numerous other States are restricting partisan considerations in districting through legislation. Other States have mandated at least some of the traditional districting criteria for their mapmakers. Some have outright prohibited partisan favoritism in redistricting. As noted, the Framers gave Congress the power to do something about partisan gerrymandering in the Elections Clause. The first bill introduced in the 116th Congress would require States to create 15-member independent commissions to draw congressional districts and would establish certain redistricting criteria, including protection for communities of interest, and ban partisan gerrymandering. H. R. 1, 116th Cong., 1st Sess., §§ 2401, 2411 (2019). . . .

No one can accuse this Court of having a crabbed view of the reach of its competence. But we have no commission to allocate political power and influence in the absence of a constitutional directive or legal standards to guide us in the exercise of such authority. "It is emphatically the province and duty of the judicial department to say what the law is." *Marbury v.*

Madison, 1 Cranch at 177. In this rare circumstance, that means our duty is to say "this is not law."

The judgments of the United States District Court for the Middle District of North Carolina and the United States District Court for the District of Maryland are vacated, and the cases are remanded with instructions to dismiss for lack of jurisdiction.

It is so ordered.

JUSTICE KAGAN, with whom JUSTICE GINSBURG, JUSTICE BREYER, and JUSTICE SOTOMAYOR join, dissenting.

For the first time ever, this Court refuses to remedy a constitutional violation because it thinks the task beyond judicial capabilities. And not just any constitutional violation. The partisan gerrymanders in these cases deprived citizens of the most fundamental of their constitutional rights: the rights to participate equally in the political process, to join with others to advance political beliefs, and to choose their political representatives. In so doing, the partisan gerrymanders here debased and dishonored our democracy, turning upside-down the core American idea that all governmental power derives from the people. These gerrymanders enabled politicians to entrench themselves in office as against voters' preferences. They promoted partisanship above respect for the popular will. They encouraged a politics of polarization and dysfunction. If left unchecked, gerrymanders like the ones here may irreparably damage our system of government.

And checking them is not beyond the courts. The majority's abdication comes just when courts across the country, including those below, have coalesced around manageable judicial standards to resolve partisan gerrymandering claims. Those standards satisfy the majority's own benchmarks. They do not require—indeed, they do not permit—courts to rely on their own ideas of electoral fairness, whether proportional representation or any other. And they limit courts to correcting only egregious gerrymanders, so judges do not become omnipresent players in the political process. But yes, the standards used here do allow—as well they should—judicial intervention in the worst-of-the-worst cases of democratic subversion, causing blatant constitutional harms. In other words, they allow courts to undo partisan gerrymanders of the kind we face today from North Carolina and Maryland. In giving such gerrymanders a pass from judicial review, the majority goes tragically wrong. . . .

The majority concedes (really, how could it not?) that gerrymandering is "incompatible with democratic principles." And therefore what? That recognition would seem to demand a response. The majority offers two ideas that might qualify as such. One is that the political process can deal with the problem—a proposition so dubious on its face that I feel secure in delaying my answer for some time. The other is that political gerrymanders have always been with us. To its credit, the majority does not frame that point as an originalist constitutional argument. After all (as the majority rightly notes), racial and residential gerrymanders were also once with us, but the Court has done something about that fact. The majority's idea instead seems to be that if we have lived with partisan gerrymanders so long, we will survive.

That complacency has no cause. Yes, partisan gerrymandering goes back to the Republic's earliest days. (As does vociferous opposition to it.) But big data and modern technology—of just the kind that the mapmakers in North Carolina and Maryland used—make today's gerrymandering altogether different from the crude linedrawing of the past. Mapmakers now have access to more granular data about party preference and voting behavior than ever before. County-level voting data has given way to precinct-level or city-block-level data; and increasingly, mapmakers avail themselves of data sets providing wide-ranging information about even individual voters. Just as important, advancements in computing technology have enabled mapmakers to put that information to use with unprecedented efficiency and precision. The effect is to make gerrymanders far more effective and durable than before, insulating politicians against all but the most titanic shifts in the political tides. These are not your grandfather's—let alone the Framers'— gerrymanders. . . . And someplace along this road, "we the people" become sovereign no longer.

Partisan gerrymandering of the kind before us not only subverts democracy (as if that weren't bad enough). It violates individuals' constitutional rights as well. That statement is not the lonesome cry of a dissenting Justice. This Court has recognized extreme partisan gerrymandering as such a violation for many years. Partisan gerrymandering operates through vote dilution—the devaluation of one citizen's vote as compared to others. That practice implicates the Fourteenth Amendment's Equal Protection Clause. The Fourteenth Amendment, we long ago recognized, "guarantees the opportunity for equal participation by all voters in the election" of legislators. *Reynolds v. Sims.* And that opportunity "can be denied by a debasement or dilution of the weight of a citizen's vote just as effectively as by wholly prohibiting the free exercise of the franchise." Based on that principle, this Court in its one-person-one-vote decisions prohibited creating districts with significantly different populations. A State could not, we explained, thus "dilut[e] the weight of votes because of place of residence." The constitutional injury in a partisan gerrymandering case is much the same, except that the dilution is based on party affiliation. . . .

And partisan gerrymandering implicates the First Amendment too. That Amendment gives its greatest protection to political beliefs, speech, and association. Yet partisan gerrymanders subject certain voters to "disfavored treatment"—again, counting their votes for less—precisely because of "their voting history [and] their expression of political views. *California Democratic Party v. Jones. . . .*

So the only way to understand the majority's opinion is as follows: In the face of grievous harm to democratic governance and flagrant infringements on individuals' rights—in the face of escalating partisan manipulation whose compatibility with this Nation's values and law no one defends—the majority declines to provide any remedy. For the first time in this Nation's history, the majority declares that it can do nothing about an acknowledged constitutional violation because it has searched high and low and cannot find a workable legal standard to apply. The majority gives two reasons for thinking that the adjudication of partisan gerrymandering claims is beyond judicial capabilities. First and foremost, the majority says, it cannot find a neutral baseline—one not based on contestable notions of political fairness—from which to measure injury. And second, the majority argues that even after establishing a baseline, a court would have no way to answer "the determinative question: 'How much is too much?'" No "discernible and manageable" standard is available, the majority claims—and so courts could willy-nilly become embroiled in fixing every districting plan.

I'll give the majority this one—and important—thing: It identifies some dangers everyone should want to avoid. Judges should not be apportioning political power based on their own vision of electoral fairness, whether proportional representation or any other. And judges should not be striking down maps left, right, and center, on the view that every smidgen of politics is a smidgen too much. Respect for state legislative processes—and restraint in the exercise of judicial authority—counsels intervention in only egregious cases.

But in throwing up its hands, the majority misses something under its nose: What it says can't be done has been done. Over the past several years, federal courts across the country—including, but not exclusively, in the decisions below—have largely converged on a standard for adjudicating partisan gerrymandering claims. And that standard does what the majority says is impossible. The standard does not use any judge-made conception of electoral fairness—either proportional representation or any other; instead, it takes as its baseline a State's own criteria of fairness, apart from partisan gain. And by requiring plaintiffs to make difficult showings relating to both purpose and effects, the standard invalidates the most extreme, but only the most extreme, partisan gerrymanders. . . .

Start with the standard the lower courts used. Both courts focused on the harm of vote dilution, though the North Carolina court mostly grounded its analysis in the Fourteenth Amendment and the Maryland court in the First. And both courts (like others around the country) used basically the same three-part test to decide whether the plaintiffs had made out a vote dilution claim. As many legal standards do, that test has three parts: (1) intent; (2) effects; and (3) causation. First, the plaintiffs challenging a districting plan must prove that state officials' "predominant purpose" in drawing a district's lines was to "entrench [their party] in power" by diluting the votes of citizens favoring its rival. Second, the plaintiffs must establish that the lines drawn in fact have the intended effect by "substantially" diluting their votes. And third, if the plaintiffs make those showings, the State must come up with a legitimate, non-partisan justification to save its map. If you are a lawyer, you know that this test looks utterly ordinary. It is the sort of thing courts work with every day. . . .

The majority does not contest the lower courts' findings; how could it? Instead, the majority says that state officials' intent to entrench their party in power is perfectly "permissible," even when it is the predominant factor in drawing district lines. But that is wrong. True enough, that the intent to inject "political considerations" into districting may not raise any constitutional concerns. . . . But when political actors have a specific and predominant intent to entrench themselves in power by manipulating district lines, that goes too far. The majority fails to discuss most of the evidence the District Courts relied on. The North Carolina plaintiffs offered a boatload of alternative districting plans—all showing that the State's map was an out-out-out-outlier. Because the Maryland gerrymander involved just one district, the evidence in that case was far simpler—but no less powerful for that. . . .

The majority claims all these findings are mere "prognostications" about the future, in which no one "can have any confidence." But the courts below did not gaze into crystal balls, as the majority tries to suggest. Their findings about these gerrymanders' effects on voters—both in the past and predictably in the future—were evidence-based, data-based, statistics-based. Knowledge-based, one might say. . . . They did not bet America's future—as today the majority does—on the idea that maps constructed with so much expertise and care to make electoral outcomes impervious to voting would somehow or other come apart. They looked at the evidence—at the facts about how these districts operated—and they could reach only one conclusion. By substantially diluting the votes of citizens favoring their rivals, the politicians of one party had succeeded in entrenching themselves in office. They had beat democracy.

The majority's broadest claim, as I've noted, is that this is a price we must pay because judicial oversight of partisan gerrymandering cannot be "politically neutral" or "manageable." Courts, the majority argues, will have to choose among contested notions of electoral fairness. And even once courts have chosen, the majority continues, they will have to decide "[h]ow much is too much?"—that is, how much deviation from the chosen "touchstone" to allow? Contrary to the majority's suggestion, the District Courts did not have to—and in fact did not—choose among competing visions of electoral fairness. That is because they did not try to compare the State's actual map to an "ideally fair" one (whether based on proportional representation or some other criterion). Instead, they looked at the difference between what the State did and what the State would have done if politicians hadn't been intent on partisan gain. Or put differently, the comparator (or baseline or touchstone) is the result not of a judge's philosophizing but of the State's own characteristics and judgments. Still more, the courts' analyses used the State's own criteria for electoral fairness—except for naked partisan gain. Under their approach, in other words, the State selected its own fairness baseline in the form of its other districting criteria. All the courts did was determine how far the State had gone off that track because of its politicians' effort to entrench themselves in office. . . .

The majority's sole response misses the point. According to the majority, "it does not make sense to use" a State's own (non-partisan) districting criteria as the baseline from which to measure partisan gerrymandering because those criteria "will vary from State to State and year to year." But that is a virtue, not a vice—a feature, not a bug. Using the criteria the State itself has chosen at the relevant time prevents any judicial predilections from affecting the analysis—exactly what the majority claims it wants. At the same time, using those criteria enables a court to measure just what it should: the extent to which the pursuit of partisan advantage—by these legislators at this moment—has distorted the State's districting decisions. . . .

The majority's "how much is too much" critique fares no better than its neutrality argument. How about the following for a first-cut answer: This much is too much. By any measure, a map that produces a greater partisan skew than any of 3,000 randomly generated maps (all with the State's political geography and districting criteria built in) reflects "too much" partisanship. Think about what I just said: The absolute worst of 3,001 possible maps. The only one that could produce a 10–3 partisan split even as Republicans got a bare majority of the statewide vote. And again: How much is too much? This much is too much: A map that without any evident non-partisan districting reason (to the contrary) shifted the composition of a district from 47% Republicans and 36% Democrats to 33% Republicans and 42% Democrats. A map that in 2011 was responsible for the largest partisan swing of a congressional district in the country. . . .

Nor is there any reason to doubt, as the majority does, the competence of courts to determine whether a district map "substantially" diphes the votes of a rival party's supporters from the everything-but-partisanship baseline described above. (Most of the majority's difficulties here really come from its idea that ideal visions set the baseline. But that is double-counting—and, as already shown, wrong to boot.) As this Court recently noted, "the law is full of instances" where a judge's decision rests on "estimating rightly . . . some matter of degree"—including the "substantial[ity]" of risk or harm. And contrary to the majority's suggestion, courts all the time make judgments about the substantiality of harm without reducing them to particular percentages. If courts are no longer competent to do so, they will have to relinquish, well, substantial portions of their docket.

And the combined inquiry used in these cases set the bar high, so that courts could intervene in the worst partisan gerrymanders, but no others. Or to say the same thing, so that courts could intervene in the kind of extreme gerrymanders that nearly every Justice for decades has thought to violate the Constitution. Illicit purpose was simple to show here only because politicians and mapmakers thought their actions could not be attacked in court. They therefore felt free to openly proclaim their intent to entrench their party in office. That the two courts below found constitutional violations does not mean their tests were unrigorous; it means that the conduct they confronted was constitutionally appalling—by even the strictest measure, inordinately partisan. . . .

This Court has long understood that it has a special responsibility to remedy violations of constitutional rights resulting from politicians' districting decisions. Over 50 years ago, we committed to providing judicial review in that sphere, recognizing as we established the one-person-one-vote rule that "our oath and our office require no less." *Reynolds.* Of course, our oath and our office require us to vindicate all constitutional rights. But the need for judicial review is at its most urgent in cases like these. "For here, politicians' incentives conflict with voters' interests, leaving citizens without any political remedy for their constitutional harms." *Gill* (Kagan, J., concurring). Those harms arise because politicians want to stay in office. No one can look to them for effective relief. And because those politicians maintain themselves in office through partisan gerrymandering, the chances for legislative reform are slight. . . .

The majority's most perplexing "solution" is to look to state courts. But what do those courts know that this Court does not? If they can develop and apply neutral and manageable standards to identify unconstitutional gerrymanders, why couldn't we?. . .

Of all times to abandon the Court's duty to declare the law, this was not the one. The practices challenged in these cases imperil our system of government. Part of the Court's role in that system is to defend its foundations. None is more important than free and fair elections. With respect but deep sadness, I dissent.

CHAPTER 3

STATE POWERS IN LIGHT OF THE COMMERCE CLAUSE

■ ■ ■

3–3 INCOMING COMMERCE

Unabridged, p. 126; add to Note 4 after *Granholm v. Heald*:

Tennessee Wine and Spirits Retailers Assn. v. Russell F. Thomas, Executive Director of the Tennessee Alcohol Beverage Commission, et al., 139 S.Ct. 2449 (2019). Tennessee imposes a two-year residency requirement on persons and businesses seeking to operate liquor stores in the state. The purpose of the requirement, as spelled out in the legislation, is to protect "the health safety, and welfare [of state residents]" which called for "a higher degree of oversight, control and accountability for individuals involved in the ownership, management and control of [liquor stores]." The Court (7–2), in an opinion by Alito, J., struck down the residency requirement as violating the Commerce Clause "[The residency requirement] blatantly favors the State's residents and has little relationship to public health and safety." The Court traced the "long and complicated history" of the dormant Commerce Clause, observing that "the proposition that the Commerce Clause by its own force restricts state protectionism is deeply rooted in our case law," and that "removing state trade barriers was a principal reason for the adoption of the Constitution." Noting that the "Import-Export Clause of Art. I, § 10, cl. 2 refers only to international trade, and that the Privileges and Immunities of Art. IV, § 2 has been interpreted not to protect corporations, "that leaves the Commerce Clause as the primary safeguard against state protectionism." Tennessee's 2-year durational residency requirement plainly favors Tennesseans over nonresidents and, as the Court concluded in *Granholm v. Heald*, is not saved by the 21st Amendment's grant of authority to states in § 2 to regulate alcohol within their borders. There is no evidence that § 2 was understood to give the states the power to enact protectionist laws; the Court has consistently endorsed the view that "the aim of § 2 was not to give States a free hand to restrict the importation of alcohol for purely protectionist purposes." The Court rejected the petitioner's "overly broad" argument that state residency requirements long predated Prohibition and were adopted by many states following ratification of the 21st Amendment. Although states have leeway to adopt measures to protect the public health and safety effects of alcohol use, states "are not licensed to adopt protectionist measures with no demonstrable connection to those interests." The residency requirement "has a highly attenuated relationship to public health or safety" and "the record is devoid of any 'concrete evidence' showing that the 2-year residency requirement actually promotes public health or safety." In any event, there are available nondiscriminatory alternatives to further those interests.

3–6   PREEMPTION

APPENDIX

AN INTRODUCTORY NOTE ON COMMERCE CLAUSE LIMITATIONS ON STATE TAXATION

Unabridged, p. 176; add at end of "Sales and Use Taxes":

In *South Dakota v. Wayfair, Inc.*, 138 S.Ct. 2080 (2018), the Court (5–4), in an opinion by Justice Kennedy, upended over fifty years of Supreme Court precedent, holding that an out-of-state company's physical presence in the taxing state is not necessary for that state to require the seller to collect and remit its sales tax. Under *National Bellas Hess, Inc. v. Department of Revenue of Ill.*, 386 U.S. 753 (1967) and *Quill Corp. v. North Dakota,* 504 U.S. 298 (1992), an out-of-state seller's liability to collect and remit the sales tax to the consumer's state depended on whether the seller had a physical presence in that state; the mere shipment of goods into the consumer's state, following an order from a catalogue, did not satisfy the physical presence requirement. Under *Bellas Hess* and *Quill*, a state may not require a business to collect its sales tax if the business lacks a physical presence in the state. Rather, the state must rely on its residents to pay a use tax on their purchases from out-of-state sellers. However, as the Court noted, "consumer compliance rates are notoriously low," and it is estimated that *Bellas Hess* and *Quill* cause states to lose between $8 and $33 billion every year.

In 2016, South Dakota, whose revenue loss from *Quill* is estimated at $48 to $58 million annually, passed a law requiring out-of-state sellers to collect and remit a sales tax as if the seller had a physical presence in the state. The law applied to sellers that on an annual basis deliver more than $100,000 of goods or services into the state or engage in 200 or more separate transactions. Pursuant to the law's provisions for expedited judicial review, South Dakota sought a declaratory judgment against respondents—three major online retailers with billions of dollars in net revenues which ships goods directly to purchasers throughout the United States, including South Dakota. Respondents have no employees or real estate in South Dakota. The trial court granted summary judgment for respondents and the state supreme court, on the authority of *Quill*, affirmed.

After surveying the general development of the Court's commerce clause jurisprudence, Justice Kennedy observed that under *Quill,* the physical presence rule "was necessary to prevent undue burdens on interstate commerce." He, along with Justices Scalia and Thomas, concurred in *Quill* on the basis of *stare decisis* alone. Justice White dissented, arguing that "there is no relationship between the physical-presence/nexus rule the Court retains and Commerce Clause considerations that allegedly justify it." But, as the majority observed, "*stare decisis* is not an inexorable command." The Cyber Age has made "far-reaching systemic and structural changes in the economy." In 1992, when *Quill* was decided, less than 2 percent of Americans had internet access; today the number is about 89 percent. In 1992, states were losing between $694 million and $3 billion per year in sales tax revenues as a result of the physical presence rule. Now estimates range from $8 to $33 billion. "Each year the physical presence rule becomes further removed from economic reality and results in significant revenue losses to the States." This rule, "as first formulated and as applied today, "is an incorrect interpretation of the Commerce Clause."

First, the physical presence rule is not necessary to create a substantial nexus between the out-of-state business and the taxing state so as to require the business to remit sales taxes. "It is an inescapable fact of modern commercial life that a substantial amount of business is transacted with no need for physical presence within a state." Moreover, the commerce clause was designed to prevent states form engaging in economic discrimination, and "not to relieve those engaged in interstate commerce from their just share of state tax burden." Nor was it the purpose of the commerce clause to "permit the Judiciary to create market distortions." Indeed, "*Quill* has come to serve as a judicially created tax shelter for businesses that decide to limit their physical presence and still sell their goods and services to a State's consumers—something that has become easier and more prevalent as technology has advanced." Also, "*Quill* treats economically identical actors differently and for arbitrary reasons." Consider a business that sells furniture online and stocks a few items of inventory in a small warehouse in Sioux City, South Dakota. The business must collect and remit a tax on all sales to South Dakota customers even though its sales have nothing to do with the warehouse. A second business, which has a major warehouse just across the border in South Sioux City, Nebraska, and maintains a sophisticated website with a virtual showroom accessible in every state, including South Dakota, would not be subject to the same tax. Finally, a tax system that "allows remote sellers to escape an obligation to remit a lawful state tax is unfair and unjust." Fairness dictates that "companies that avail themselves of the State's benefits bear an equal share of the burden of tax collection." "It is essential to public confidence in the tax system that the Court avoid creating inequitable exceptions." The physical presence rule of *Quill* and *Bellas Hess* "is unsound and incorrect" and these decisions are overruled.

Chief Justice Roberts, joined by Breyer, Sotomayor, and Kagan, JJ., dissented. While agreeing that *Quill* and *Bellas Hess* were wrongly decided, they argued that any alteration of the rules governing such a significant and vibrant part of the national economy should be undertaken by Congress. The Court "proceeds with an inexplicable sense of urgency." It "breezily disregards the costs that its decision will impose on retailers." And the burden "will fall disproportionately on small businesses." Congress is in a much better position to consider and balance the competing interests than the Court, and after investigation may decide that current trends might expand tax revenues and obviate the need for an abrupt policy shift with adverse consequences on e-commerce. "The Court should not act on this important question of current economic policy, solely to expiate a mistake it made over 50 years ago."

CHAPTER 4

FEDERAL POWERS UNDER THE COMMERCE CLAUSE

■ ■ ■

4–1   THE PRE-1937 CASES

Unabridged, p. 209; add to footnote 2:

United States v. Gundy, 139 S.Ct. 2116, ___ L.Ed.2d ___ (2019), Section 20913(d) of the Sex Offender Registration and Notification Act (SORNA) requires a broad range of sex offenders to register and authorizes the Attorney General to prescribe rules for their registration, particularly to pre-Act offenders who failed to register. Kagan, J., joined by Ginsburg, Breyer, and Sotomayor, JJ, concluded that the provision does not violate the non-delegation doctrine. The delegation does not authorize the Attorney General to do whatever he wants to do with pre-Act offenders, as the defendant claims. The provision requires action by the Attorney General as soon as feasible, given the transition difficulties in implementing the new statute. Section 20913(d) falls well within constitutional bounds and is distinctly "small bore" compared to delegations the Court has upheld in the past. Alito, concurring in the judgment, concluded that he cannot say the statute lacks an adequate standard under the approach the Court has taken for 84 years, but he would reconsider that approach in an appropriate case. Gorsuch, J., joined by Roberts, C.J. and Thomas, J., dissented arguing that the statute is an "extraconstitutional arrangement" that violates separation of powers by allowing Congress, which has exclusive law-making power, "to endow the nation's chief prosecutor with the power to write his own criminal code governing the lives of a half-million citizens." Kavanaugh, J., took no part in the decision.

4–4   MODERN COMMERCE CLAUSE CASES

Unabridged, p. 302; add to end of *Notes*, new Note 8:

Abridged, p. 264; add to end of *Notes*, new Note 8:

8.   *King v. Burwell*, 576 U.S. ___, 135 S.Ct. 2480, 192 L.Ed.2d 483 (2015). This case is significant although it relates to statutory interpretation, not the Commerce Clause. The Affordable Care Act (ACA) provides that if a state sets up a "qualified health exchange," then the insureds qualify for generous federal subsidies. If a state refuses to do that, the law authorizes the Secretary of Health and Human Services (HHS) to set up Federal Exchanges. No provision of the ACA offers any tax subsidies for *federally* created (as opposed to *state* created) Health Exchanges. If the state refuses to create a Health Exchange, that state's citizens do not receive these financial subsidies, but they still have to pay federal taxes that finance the subsidies that residents in other states (those with state-created Exchanges) will receive.

No section of the ACA defines "State" to include the federal government; other sections define "State" to include the 50 states, the District of Columbia, and U.S. territories, e.g., Guam. To the surprise of many ACA supporters, only 16 States and the District of Columbia established their own Exchanges. Given that so many states did not enact qualified exchanges, the IRS issued a regulation interpreting the relevant language to provide that "regardless of whether the Exchange is established and operated by a State . . . or by HHS," the subsidies are available. Roberts, C.J. for the Court (6 to 3), held that Congress did not intend to delegate to the IRS the power to issue such an interpretation but since the statutory language is ambiguous, the Court will interpret it. The Court conceded that "The Affordable Care Act contains more than a few examples of inartful drafting" and "arguments about the plain meaning of Section 36B are strong." Nonetheless, in light of the "broader structure of the Act," these subsidies are necessary and that "compels us to reject petitioners' interpretation because it would destabilize the individual insurance market in any State with a Federal Exchange, and likely create the very 'death spirals' that Congress designed the Act to avoid." Because the Court did not accept the Solicitor General's argument to defer to the IRS, a future IRS regulation under a different Administration cannot change the interpretation of this law.

Scalia, J., joined by Thomas & Alito, JJ., dissented. "The Court holds that when the [ACA] says 'Exchange established by the State' it means 'Exchange established by the State or the Federal Government.' That is of course quite absurd, and the Court's 21 pages of explanation make it no less so." Words have no meaning if an Exchange "*not* established by a State is 'established by the State.'" "We lack the prerogative to repair laws that do not work out in practice, just as the people lack the ability to throw us out of office if they dislike the solutions we concoct." The Court attempts "to palm off the pertinent statutory phrase as 'inartful drafting'" but it "does not pretend" that there is any "drafting error on the face of § 36B." For this Court, "normal rules of interpretation seem always to yield to the overriding principle of the present Court: The Affordable Care Act must be saved." The Court has engaged in "interpretive jiggery-pokery," and thus, "We should start calling this law SCOTUScare." (SCOTUS stands for Supreme Court of the United States.)*

---

*   For further discussion see Rotunda, *King v. Burwell and the Rise of the Administrative State*, 23 U. MIAMI BUSINESS REV. 267 (2015).

4–5   MODERN TENTH AMENDMENT RESTRICTIONS ON THE COMMERCE POWER

Unabridged, p. 334; before *Notes,* add new case and *Notes*:

Abridged, p. 285; before *Notes,* add new case and *Notes*:

MURPHY v. NATIONAL COLLEGIATE ATHLETIC ASSOCIATION, ET AL.

138 S.Ct. 1461, 200 L.Ed.2d 854 (2018).

JUSTICE ALITO delivered the opinion of the Court.

Americans have never been of one mind about gambling, and attitudes have swung back and forth. By the end of the 19th century, gambling was largely banned throughout the country, but beginning in the 1920s and 1930s, laws prohibiting gambling were gradually loosened. . . . Sports gambling, however, has long had strong opposition. Opponents argue that it is particularly addictive and especially attractive to young people with a strong interest in sports, and in the past gamblers corrupted and seriously damaged the reputation of professional and amateur sports. Apprehensive about the potential effects of sports gambling, professional sports leagues and the National Collegiate Athletic Association (NCAA) long opposed legalization. By the 1990s, there were signs that the trend that had brought about the legalization of many other forms of gambling might extend to sports gambling, and this sparked federal efforts to stem the tide. Opponents of sports gambling turned to the legislation now before us, the Professional and Amateur Sports Protection Act (PASPA). . . . PASPA's most important provision, part of which is directly at issue in these cases, makes it "unlawful" for a State or any of its subdivisions "to sponsor, operate, advertise, promote, license, or authorize by law or compact . . . a lottery, sweepstakes, or other betting, gambling, or wagering scheme based . . . on" competitive sporting events. § 3702(1). In parallel, § 3702(2) makes it "unlawful" for "a person to sponsor, operate, advertise, or promote" those same gambling schemes—but only if this is done "pursuant to the law or compact of a governmental entity." PASPA does not make sports gambling a federal crime (and thus was not anticipated to impose a significant law enforcement burden on the Federal Government). Instead, PASPA allows the Attorney General, as well as professional and amateur sports organizations, to bring civil actions to enjoin violations. § 3703.

At the time of PASPA's adoption, a few jurisdictions allowed some form of sports gambling. In Nevada, sports gambling was legal in casinos, and three States hosted sports lotteries or allowed sports pools. PASPA contains "grandfather" provisions allowing these activities to continue. Another provision gave New Jersey the option of legalizing sports gambling in Atlantic City—provided that it did so within one year of the law's effective date.

New Jersey did not take advantage of this special option, but by 2011, with Atlantic City facing stiff competition, the State had a change of heart. New Jersey voters approved an amendment to the State Constitution making it lawful for the legislature to authorize sports gambling, and in 2012 the legislature enacted a law doing just that.

The 2012 Act quickly came under attack. The major professional sports leagues and the NCAA brought an action in federal court against the New Jersey Governor and other state officials (hereinafter New Jersey), seeking to enjoin the new law on the ground that it violated PASPA. In response, the State argued, among other things, that PASPA unconstitutionally infringed the State's sovereign authority to end its sports gambling ban. In making this argument, the State relied primarily on two cases, *New York v. United States,* (1992), and *Printz v. United States,* (1997), in which we struck down federal laws based on what has been dubbed the "anticommandeering" principle. In *New York,* we held that a federal law unconstitutionally ordered the State to regulate in accordance with federal standards, and in *Printz,* we found that another federal statute unconstitutionally compelled state officers to enforce federal law.

Relying on these cases, New Jersey argued that PASPA is similarly flawed because it regulates a State's exercise of its lawmaking power by prohibiting it from modifying or repealing its laws prohibiting sports gambling. The plaintiffs countered that PASPA is critically different from the commandeering cases because it does not command the States to take any affirmative act. Without an affirmative federal command to *do* something, the plaintiffs insisted, there can be no claim of commandeering.

The District Court found no anticommandeering violation, and a divided panel of the Third Circuit affirmed. The panel thought it significant that PASPA does not impose any affirmative command. In the words of the panel, "PASPA does not require or coerce the states to lift a finger." The panel recognized that an affirmative command (for example, "Do not repeal") can often be phrased as a prohibition ("Repeal is prohibited"), but the panel did not interpret PASPA as prohibiting the repeal of laws outlawing sports gambling. A repeal, it thought, would not amount to "authoriz[ation]" and thus would fall outside the scope of § 3702(1). "[T]he lack of an affirmative prohibition of an activity," the panel wrote, "does not mean it is affirmatively authorized by law. The right to do that which is not prohibited derives not from the authority of the state but from the inherent rights of the people." New Jersey filed a petition for a writ of certiorari, raising the anticommandeering issue.

Opposing certiorari, the United States told this Court that PASPA does not require New Jersey "to leave in place the state-law prohibitions against sports gambling that it had chosen to adopt prior to PASPA's enactment. To the contrary, New Jersey is free to repeal those prohibitions in whole or in part."

Picking up on the suggestion that a partial repeal would be allowed, the New Jersey Legislature enacted the law now before us. The 2014 Act declares that it is not to be interpreted as causing the State to authorize, license, sponsor, operate, advertise, or promote sports gambling. Instead, it is framed as a repealer. Specifically, it repeals the provisions of state law prohibiting sports gambling insofar as they concerned the "placement and acceptance of wagers" on sporting events by persons 21 years of age or older at a horseracing track or a casino or gambling house in Atlantic City. The new law also specified that the repeal was effective only as to wagers on sporting events not involving a New Jersey college team or a collegiate event taking place in the State.

Predictably, the same plaintiffs promptly commenced a new action in federal court. They won in the District Court, and the case was eventually heard by the Third Circuit sitting en banc. The en banc court affirmed, finding that the new law, no less than the old one, violated PASPA by "author[izing]" sports gambling. The court was unmoved by the New Jersey Legislature's "artful[ ]" attempt to frame the 2014 Act as a repealer. Looking at what the law "actually does," the court concluded that it constitutes an authorization because it "selectively remove[s] a prohibition on sports wagering in a manner that permissively channels wagering activity to particular locations or operators." The court observed that a partial repeal that allowed only "*de minimis*" wagers between friends and family would not have nearly the type of authorizing effect" that it found in the 2014 Act, and it added: "We need not . . . articulate a line whereby a partial repeal of a sports wagering ban amounts to an authorization under PASPA, if indeed such a line could be drawn." Having found that the 2014 Act violates PASPA's prohibition of state authorization of sports gambling schemes, the court went on to hold that this prohibition does not contravene the anticommandeering principle because it "does not command states to take affirmative actions."

Before considering the constitutionality of the PASPA provision prohibiting States from "author[izing]" sports gambling, we first examine its meaning. The parties advance dueling interpretations, and this dispute has an important bearing on the constitutional issue that we must decide. Petitioners argue that the anti-authorization provision requires States to maintain their existing laws against sports gambling without alteration. One of the accepted meanings of the term "authorize," they point out, is "permit." They therefore contend that any state law that has the effect of permitting sports gambling, including a law totally or partially repealing a prior prohibition, amounts to an authorization. Respondents interpret the provision more narrowly. They claim that the primary definition of "authorize" requires affirmative action. To authorize, they maintain, means " '[t]o empower; to give a right or authority to act; to endow with authority.' " And this, they say, is precisely what the Act does: It empowers a defined group of entities, and it endows them with the authority to conduct sports gambling operations. . . .

In our view, petitioners' interpretation is correct: When a State completely or partially repeals old laws banning sports gambling, it "authorize[s]" that activity. This is clear when the state-law landscape at the time of PASPA's enactment is taken into account. At that time, all forms of sports gambling were illegal in the great majority of States, and in that context, the competing definitions offered by the parties lead to the same conclusion. The repeal of a state law banning sports gambling not only "permits" sports gambling (petitioners' favored definition); it also gives those now free to conduct a sports betting operation the "right or authority to act"; it "empowers" them (respondents' and the United States's definition). The concept of state "authorization" makes sense only against a backdrop of prohibition or regulation. A State is not regarded as authorizing everything that it does not prohibit or regulate. No one would use the term in that way. For example, no one would say that a State "authorizes" its residents to brush their teeth or eat apples or sing in the shower. We commonly speak of state authorization only if the activity in question would otherwise be restricted. . . .

The anticommandeering doctrine may sound arcane, but it is simply the expression of a fundamental structural decision incorporated into the Constitution, i.e., the decision to withhold from Congress the power to issue orders directly to the States. When the original States declared their independence, they claimed the powers inherent in sovereignty—in the words of the Declaration of Independence, the authority "to do all . . . Acts and Things which Independent States may of right do." ¶ 32. The Constitution limited but did not abolish the sovereign powers of the States, which retained "a residuary and inviolable sovereignty." The Federalist No. 39, p. 245 (C. Rossiter ed. 1961). Thus, both the Federal Government and the States wield sovereign powers, and that is why our system of government is said to be one of "dual sovereignty.". . .

The legislative powers granted to Congress are sizable, but they are not unlimited. The Constitution confers on Congress not plenary legislative power but only certain enumerated powers. Therefore, all other legislative power is reserved for the States, as the Tenth Amendment confirms. And conspicuously absent from the list of powers given to Congress is the power to issue direct orders to the governments of the States. The anticommandeering doctrine simply represents the recognition of this limit on congressional authority.

Although the anticommandeering principle is simple and basic, it did not emerge in our cases until relatively recently, when Congress attempted in a few isolated instances to extend its authority in unprecedented ways. The pioneering case was *New York v. United States*, which concerned a federal law that required a State, under certain circumstances, either to "take title" to low-level radioactive waste or to "regulat[e] according to the instructions of Congress." [T]he Court held the provision was unconstitutional because "the Constitution does not empower Congress to subject state governments to this type of instruction. . . We have always understood that even where Congress has the authority under the Constitution to pass laws requiring or prohibiting certain acts, it lacks the power directly to compel the States to require or prohibit those acts. . . Congress may not simply commandee[r] the legislative processes of the States by directly compelling them to enact and enforce a federal regulatory program." Five years after New York, the Court applied the same principles to a federal statute requiring state and local law enforcement officers to perform background checks and related tasks in connection with applications for handgun licenses. *Printz*. Holding this provision unconstitutional, the Court put the point succinctly: "The Federal Government" may not "command the States' officers, or those of their political subdivisions, to administer or enforce a federal regulatory program.". . .

Our opinions in *New York* and *Printz* explained why adherence to the anticommandeering principle is important. Without attempting a complete survey, we mention several reasons that are significant here. First, the rule serves as "one of the Constitution's structural protections of liberty." *Printz*, "The Constitution does not protect the sovereignty of States for the benefit of the States or state governments as abstract political entities." *New York*. "To the contrary, the Constitution divides authority between federal and state governments for the protection of individuals. . . .[A] healthy balance of power between the States and the Federal Government [reduces] the risk of tyranny and abuse from either front."

Second, the anticommandeering rule promotes political accountability. When Congress itself regulates, the responsibility for the benefits and burdens of the regulation is apparent. Voters who like or dislike the effects of the regulation know who to credit or blame. By contrast, if a State imposes regulations only because it has been commanded to do so by Congress, responsibility is blurred. Third, the anticommandeering principle prevents Congress from shifting the costs of regulation to the States. If Congress enacts a law and requires enforcement by the Executive Branch, it must appropriate the funds needed to administer the program. It is pressured to weigh the expected benefits of the program against its costs. But if Congress can compel the States to enact and enforce its program, Congress need not engage in any such analysis.

The PASPA provision at issue here—prohibiting state authorization of sports gambling—violates the anticommandeering rule. That provision unequivocally dictates what a state legislature may and may not do. And this is true under either our interpretation or that advocated by respondents and the United States. In either event, state legislatures are put under the direct control of Congress. It is as if federal officers were installed in state legislative chambers and were armed with the authority to stop legislators from voting on any offending proposals. A more direct affront to state sovereignty is not easy to imagine. Neither respondents nor the United States contends that Congress can compel a State to enact legislation, but they say that prohibiting a State from enacting new laws is another matter. Noting that the laws challenged in *New York* and *Printz* "told states what they must do instead of what they must not do," respondents contend that commandeering occurs "only when Congress goes beyond precluding state action and affirmatively commands it." This distinction is empty. It was a matter of happenstance that the laws challenged in *New York* and *Printz* commanded "affirmative" action as opposed to imposing a prohibition. The basic principle—that Congress cannot issue direct orders to state legislatures—applies in either event. . . .

The legalization of sports gambling is a controversial subject. Supporters argue that legalization will produce revenue for the States and critically weaken illegal sports betting operations, which are often run by organized crime. Opponents contend that legalizing sports gambling will hook the young on gambling, encourage people of modest means to squander their savings and earnings, and corrupt professional and college sports. The legalization of sports gambling requires an important policy choice, but the choice is not ours to make. Congress can regulate sports gambling directly, but if it elects not to do so, each State is free to act on its own. Our job is to interpret the law Congress has enacted and decide whether it is consistent with the Constitution. PASPA is not. PASPA "regulate [s] state governments' regulation" of their citizens. *New York*. The Constitution gives Congress no such power. The judgment of the Third Circuit is reversed.

It is so ordered.

NOTES

After finding the "authorization" provision unconstitutional, the Court considered whether the other provisions in PAPSA prohibiting states from "operating," "sponsoring," or "promoting" sports gambling; prohibiting private individuals from "operating," "sponsoring," or "promoting" sports gambling; and prohibiting advertising of sports gambling, were severable from the "authorization" provision. The Court concluded they were not severable. Under the test for severability, "it must be evident that Congress would not have enacted those provisions which are within its power independently of those which are not." So, for example, legalizing sports gambling in privately owned casinos while prohibiting state-run sports lotteries "would have seemed exactly backwards." The provisions barring private actors from operating gambling schemes "were obviously meant to work together with the provisions that impose similar restrictions on government entities." These provisions "were meant to be deployed in tandem to stop what PAPSA aimed to prevent: state legalization of sports gambling." Severing these provisions would implement a "perverse policy" and produce a "weird result." Thomas, J., concurring, criticized as "dubious" the severability doctrine because it invites courts "to make a nebulous inquiry into hypothetical congressional intent." Ginsburg, J., joined by Breyer & Sotomayor, JJ., dissented. They argued that the Court "wields an ax to cut down [the statute] instead of using a scalpel to trim the statute." Even if Congress could not constitutionally prohibit a state from authorizing sports gambling, Congress would have wanted to keep sports gambling from spreading by prohibiting states and individuals from operating sports gambling schemes, which is well within Congress's power. Which interpretation of Congress's intent makes more sense?

CHAPTER 5

THE PRESIDENT AND CONGRESS

■ ■ ■

5–1 THE FOUNDATIONS OF THE FOREIGN AFFAIRS POWER

5–1.1 HISTORICAL FOUNDATIONS

Unabridged, p. 353; add to end of *Notes*, new Note 6:

Abridged, p. 302; add to end of *Notes*, new Note 6:

6. *Zivotofsky v. Kerry*, 576 U.S. ___, 135 S.Ct. 2076, 192 L.Ed.2d 83 (2015). Zivotofsky was born to United States citizens living in Jerusalem. His parents, on his behalf, sued the Secretary of State for declaratory and injunctive relief, arguing that the child was entitled—pursuant to the Foreign Relations Authorization Act (FRAA)—to have "Israel" listed as his place of birth on his U.S. passport. Instead, pursuant to State Department policy, the passport would list only "Jerusalem." Justice Kennedy, for the Court, held (6 to 3) that this law violated the President's exclusive power to recognize foreign nations and governments, Art. II, § 3. The Executive Branch's longstanding position is that the United States "does not recognize any country as having sovereignty over Jerusalem."

Thomas, J. (concurring in the judgment and dissenting in part) concluded that § 214(d) was unconstitutional "insofar as it directs the President, contrary to his wishes, to list 'Israel' as the place of birth of Jerusalem-born citizens on their passports." That is because the "President has long regulated passports under his residual foreign affairs power." However, "§ 214(d) poses no such problem insofar as it regulates consular reports of birth abroad." "The regulation of these reports does not fall within the President's foreign affairs powers, but within Congress' enumerated powers under the Naturalization and Necessary and Proper Clauses."

Roberts, C.J., joined by Alito, J., dissented. "Never before has this Court accepted a President's direct defiance of an Act of Congress in the field of foreign affairs. We have instead stressed that the President's power reaches 'its lowest ebb, when he contravenes the express will of Congress, 'for what is at stake is the equilibrium established by our constitutional system,'" quoting Justice Jackson's concurrence in *Youngstown*. Scalia, J., joined by Roberts, C.J., & Alito, J., also dissented, noting that eleven of the powers that Article I, § 8 grants Congress deal in some way with foreign affairs. Section

214(d) "has nothing to do with recognition" of a foreign sovereign. It does not require the "Secretary to make a formal declaration about Israel's sovereignty over Jerusalem." Birthplace designation on a passport has nothing to do with exchanges of ambassadors.

5–3 ADMISSION AND DEPORTATION OF ALIENS

Unabridged, p. 406; add to *Notes*, new Note 4:

4. *Sessions v. Morales-Santana,* 582 U.S. ___, 137 S.Ct. 1678, 198 L.Ed.2d 150 (2017). Son born abroad to an unwed citizen father and a non-citizen mother sought to reopen his removal proceedings to evaluate his claim of derivative citizenship. The Immigration and Nationality Act allows for acquisition of U.S. citizenship from birth by a child born abroad, when one parent is a U.S. citizen and the other is not, under certain circumstances. If the U.S.-citizen parent must have ten years' physical presence in the United States prior to the child's birth, "at least five of which were after attaining" age 14. However, if the child seeks citizenship through his unwed U.S.-citizen mother, the mother can transmit her citizenship to her child born abroad if she has lived continuously in the United States for just one year prior to the child's birth. The Government sought to remove Morales-Santana based on several criminal convictions, and treated him as alien because he sought citizenship through his citizen-father. He would have qualified if the law treated his citizen-father the same as the citizen-mother.

Ginsburg, J., for the Court, held that the gender line that Congress drew violates the Fifth Amendment's requirement that the Government accord to all persons "the equal protection of the laws." The Court distinguished *Fiallo v. Bell*, 430 U.S. 787, 97 S.Ct. 1473, 52 L.Ed.2d 50 (1977) because *Fiallo* involved entry preferences for alien children; the case did not present a claim of U.S. citizenship. This sex-based distinction between unwed fathers and unwed mothers (premised on the archaic view that unwed fathers care less about their children than unwed mothers do) is unconstitutional.

However, the Court stated that it is not equipped to convert the one-year exception for unwed mothers into the main rule. Congress must decide that issue. Ordinarily "the preferred rule" is to extend favorable treatment to the excluded class rather than withdrawing favorable treatment from the favored class. However, extending the one-year rule for unwed mothers to unwed fathers would displace Congress' general rule that requires longer physical presence. Therefore, the Court held it would adopt the rule that Congress would likely have chosen—to apply the longer five-year requirement of the general rule prospectively to children born to unwed citizen mothers. "Going forward, Congress may address the issue and settle on a uniform prescription that neither favors nor disadvantages any person on the basis of gender. In the interim, as the Government suggests, § 1401(a)(7)'s now-five-year requirement should apply, prospectively, to children born to unwed U.S.-citizen mothers."

Thomas, J., joined by Alito, J., concurred in the judgment, and said, "I am skeptical that we even have the 'power to provide relief of the sort requested in this suit—namely, conferral of citizenship on a basis other than that prescribed by Congress.' "

Unabridged, p. 406; at the end of *Notes*, add new case:

TRUMP V. HAWAII
138 S.Ct. 2392, 201 L.Ed.2d 775 (2018).

[Shortly after taking office, President Trump signed Executive Order No. 13769 (EO-1) directing the Secretary of Homeland Security to examine the adequacy of information provided by foreign governments about their nationals seeking to enter the United States. Pending this review the order suspended for 90 days the entry of foreign nationals from seven countries—Iran, Iraq, Libya, Somalia, Sudan, Syria, and Yemen—as posing heightened terrorism risks. The order was temporarily blocked by the federal district court in Washington and the Ninth Circuit denied the government's request for a stay. *Washington v. Trump,* 847 F.3d 1151 (2017)(*per curiam*). The President revoked EO-1 and replaced it with a new Executive Order No. 13780 (EO-2) which cited the need to reduce the risk that dangerous individuals would enter the U.S. without adequate vetting. EO-2 temporarily restricted entry of foreign nations from six of the countries covered by EO-1 because each "is a state sponsor of terrorism." District Courts in Maryland and Hawaii entered nationwide preliminary injunctions barring enforcement of the entry suspensions and the respective Courts of Appeals upheld those injunctions. *International Refugee Assistance Project (IRAP) v. Trump,* 857 F.3d 554 (4th Cir. 2017); *Hawaii v. Trump,* 859 F.3d 741 (9th Cir. 2017)(*per curiam*). The Supreme Court granted certiorari and stayed the injunctions, allowing some of the entry suspensions to go into effect. *Trump v. IRAP,* 137 S.Ct. 2080 (2017)(*per curiam*). Since the restrictions in EO-2 expired before the Supreme Court took any action, the Court vacated the lower court decisions as moot. *Trump v. IRAP,* 138 S.Ct. 353 (2017); *Trump v. Hawaii,* 138 S.Ct. 377 (2017).

On September 24, 2017, the President issued Proclamation No. 9645, 82 Fed. Reg. 45161 which sought to improve vetting procedures used to identify whether foreign nationals of eight foreign countries presented "public safety threats," and imposed entry restrictions on nationals from these countries. The Proclamation described how the foreign states were selected for inclusion using a "baseline" to determine a county's risk profile, which included the extent to which the foreign state ensures the integrity of travel documents; discloses information about criminal history and suspected terrorist links; and whether the foreign state is a known or potential terrorist safe haven. Following a 50-day review period, the Secretary of Homeland Security identified eight countries—Chad, Iran, Iraq, Libya, North Korea, Syria, Venezuela, and Yemen—which were found to be deficient under the risk profile and recommended the President impose entry restrictions on nationals from all of those countries except Iraq. The President adopted the recommendations and issued his Proclamation, which imposed a range of restrictions on entry, and contained exemptions for permanent residents and foreign nations who have been granted asylum, and case-by-case waivers for nationals demonstrating undue hardship.

Plaintiffs State of Hawaii, three individuals, and the Muslim Association of Hawaii, challenged the Proclamation, claiming it violates provisions in the Immigration and Nationality Act and violates the Establishment Clause of the First Amendment. The District Court granted a nationwide preliminary injunction, concluding that the Proclamation violated the INA on two grounds: first, the President did not make sufficient findings that the entry of the covered foreign nationals would be detrimental to the national security interest and second, because the policy discriminates against immigrant visa applicants on the basis of nationality. The Ninth Circuit, at the government's request, granted a partial stay with respect to foreign nationals who lack a bona fide relationship with the United States. The Supreme Court stayed the injunction in full pending disposition of the government's appeal. The Court of Appeals affirmed. 878 F.3d 662 (2017). The court held that the Proclamation exceeds the President's power since § 1182(f) authorizes only a "temporary" suspension in response to "exigencies" that "Congress would be ill-equipped to address;" the Proclamation conflicts with "the INA's finely reticulated regulatory scheme" by addressing "matters of immigration already passed up[on by Congress;" and the entry restrictions contravene the prohibition on nationality-based discrimination in the issuance of immigration visas. The court did not reach plaintiffs' Establishment Clause claim].

CHIEF JUSTICE ROBERTS delivered the opinion of the Court. . . .

II

Before addressing the merits of plaintiffs' statutory claims, we consider whether we have authority to do so. The Government argues that plaintiffs' challenge to the Proclamation under the INA is not justiciable. Relying on the doctrine of consular nonreviewability, the Government contends that because aliens have no "claim of right" to enter the United States, and because exclusion of aliens is "a fundamental act of sovereignty" by the political branches, review of an exclusion decision "is not within the province of any court, unless expressly authorized by law." *United States ex rel. Knauff v. Shaughnessy*, 338 U.S. 537, 542–543, 70 S.Ct. 309, 94 L.Ed. 317 (1950). The justiciability of plaintiffs' challenge under the INA presents a difficult question. The Government does not argue that the doctrine of consular nonreviewability goes to the Court's jurisdiction, nor does it point to any provision of the INA that expressly strips the Court of jurisdiction over plaintiffs' claims. As a result, we may assume without deciding that plaintiffs' statutory claims are reviewable, notwithstanding consular nonreviewability or any other statutory nonreviewability issue, and we proceed on that basis.

III

The INA establishes numerous grounds on which an alien abroad may be inadmissible to the United States and ineligible for a visa. See, e.g., 8 U.S.C. §§ 1182(a)(1) (health-related grounds), (a)(2) (criminal history), (a)(3)(B) (terrorist activities), (a)(3)(C) (foreign policy grounds). Congress has also delegated to the President authority to suspend or restrict the entry of aliens in certain circumstances. The principal source of that authority, § 1182(f), states:

> "Whenever the President finds that the entry of any aliens or of any class of aliens into the United States would be detrimental to the interests of the United States, he may by proclamation, and for such period as he shall deem necessary, suspend the entry of all aliens or any class of aliens as immigrants or nonimmigrants, or impose on the entry of aliens any restrictions he may deem to be appropriate."

. . .The Proclamation falls well within this comprehensive delegation. The sole prerequisite set forth in § 1182(f) is that the President "find[ ]" that the entry of the covered aliens "would be detrimental to the interests of the United States." The President has undoubtedly fulfilled that requirement here. He first ordered DHS and other agencies to conduct a comprehensive evaluation of every single country's compliance with the information and risk assessment baseline. The President then issued a Proclamation setting forth extensive findings describing how deficiencies in the practices of select foreign governments—several of which are state sponsors of terrorism—deprive the Government of "sufficient information to assess the risks [those countries' nationals] pose to the United States." Proclamation § 1(h)(i). Based on that review, the President found that it was in the national interest to restrict entry of aliens who could not be vetted with adequate information—both to protect national security and public safety, and to induce improvement by their home countries. The Proclamation therefore "craft[ed] . . . country-specific restrictions that would be most likely to encourage cooperation given each country's distinct circumstances," while securing the Nation "until such time as improvements occur."

Plaintiffs believe that these findings are insufficient. They argue, as an initial matter, that the Proclamation fails to provide a persuasive rationale for why nationality alone renders the covered foreign nationals a security risk. And they further discount the President's stated concern about deficient vetting because the Proclamation allows many aliens from the designated countries to enter on nonimmigrant visas. . . . [P]laintiffs' attacks on the sufficiency of the President's findings cannot be sustained. The 12-page Proclamation—which thoroughly describes the process, agency evaluations, and recommendations underlying the President's chosen restrictions—is more detailed than any prior order a President has issued under § 1182(f). Contrast Presidential Proclamation No. 6958, 3 C.F.R. 133 (1996) (President Clinton) (explaining in one sentence why suspending entry of members of the Sudanese government and armed forces "is in the foreign policy interests of the United States"); Presidential Proclamation No. 4865, 3 C.F.R. 50–51 (1981) (President Reagan) (explaining in five sentences why measures to curtail "the continuing illegal migration by sea of large numbers of undocumented aliens into the southeastern United States" are "necessary"). And when the President adopts "a preventive measure . . . in the context of international affairs and national security," he is "not required to conclusively link all of the pieces in the puzzle before [courts] grant weight to [his] empirical conclusions." *Holder v. Humanitarian Law Project*, 561 U.S. 1, 35, 130 S.Ct. 2705, 177 L.Ed.2d 355 (2010).

The Proclamation also comports with the remaining textual limits in § 1182(f). [T]he Proclamation makes clear that its "conditional restrictions" will remain in force only so long as necessary to "address" the identified "inadequacies and risks" within the covered nations. Indeed, after the initial review period, the President determined that Chad had made sufficient improvements to its identity-management protocols, and he accordingly lifted the entry suspension on its nationals. See Proclamation No. 9723, 83 Fed. Reg. 15937. Finally, the Proclamation properly identifies a "class of aliens"—nationals of select countries—whose entry is suspended. In short, the language of § 1182(f) is clear, and the Proclamation does not exceed any textual limit on the President's authority.

Confronted with this "facially broad grant of power," plaintiffs focus their attention on statutory structure and legislative purpose. They seek support in, first, the immigration scheme reflected in the INA as a whole, and, second, the legislative history of § 1182(f) and historical practice. Neither argument justifies departing from the clear text of the statute. Plaintiffs' structural argument starts with the premise that § 1182(f) does not give the President authority to countermand Congress's considered policy judgments. The President, they say, may supplement the INA, but he cannot supplant it. And in their view, the Proclamation falls in the latter category because Congress has already specified a two-part solution to the problem of aliens seeking entry from countries that do not share sufficient information with the United States. First, Congress designed an individualized vetting system that places the burden on the alien to prove his admissibility. See § 1361. Second, instead of banning the entry of nationals from particular countries, Congress sought to encourage information sharing through a Visa Waiver Program offering fast-track admission for countries that cooperate with the United States. See § 1187.

We may assume that § 1182(f) does not allow the President to expressly override particular provisions of the INA. But plaintiffs have not identified any conflict between the statute and the Proclamation that would implicitly bar the President from addressing deficiencies in the Nation's vetting system. To the contrary, the Proclamation supports Congress's individualized approach for determining admissibility. The INA sets forth various inadmissibility grounds based on connections to terrorism and criminal history, but those provisions can only work when the consular officer has sufficient (and sufficiently reliable) information to make that determination. The Proclamation promotes the effectiveness of the vetting process by helping to ensure the availability of such information. . . .

Nor is there a conflict between the Proclamation and the Visa Waiver Program. The Program allows travel without a visa for short-term visitors from 38 countries that have entered into a "rigorous security partnership" with the United States. DHS, U.S. Visa Waiver Program (Apr. 6, 2016). Eligibility for that partnership involves "broad and consequential assessments of [the country's] foreign security standards and operations." Ibid. A foreign government must (among other things) undergo a comprehensive evaluation of its "counterterrorism, law enforcement, immigration enforcement, passport security, and border management capabilities," often including "operational site inspections of airports, seaports, land borders, and passport production and issuance facilities." Ibid. Congress's decision to authorize a benefit for "many of America's closest allies," ibid., did not implicitly foreclose the Executive from imposing tighter restrictions on nationals of certain high-risk countries. The Visa Waiver Program creates a special exemption for citizens of countries that maintain exemplary security standards and offer "reciprocal [travel] privileges" to United States citizens. 8 U.S.C. § 1187(a)(2)(A). But in establishing a select partnership covering less than 20% of the countries in the world, Congress did not address what requirements should govern the entry of nationals from the vast majority of countries that fall short of that gold standard—particularly those nations presenting heightened terrorism concerns. Nor did Congress attempt to determine—as the multi-agency review process did—whether those high-risk countries provide a minimum baseline of information to adequately vet their nationals. Fairly read, the provision vests authority in the President to impose additional limitations on entry beyond the grounds for exclusion set forth in the INA—including in response to circumstances that might affect the vetting system or other "interests of the United States." Because plaintiffs do not point to any contradiction with another provision of the INA, the President has not exceeded his authority under § 1182(f).

Plaintiffs seek to locate additional limitations on the scope of § 1182(f) in the statutory background and legislative history. Given the clarity of the text, we need not consider such extra-textual evidence. See *State Farm Fire & Casualty Co. v. United States ex rel. Rigsby*, 580 U.S. ___, ___, 137 S.Ct. 436, 444, 196 L.Ed.2d 340 (2016). At any rate, plaintiffs' evidence supports the plain meaning of the provision. Drawing on legislative debates over § 1182(f), plaintiffs suggest that the President's suspension power should be limited to exigencies where it would be difficult for Congress to react promptly. Precursor provisions enacted during the First and Second World Wars confined the President's exclusion authority to times of "war" and "national emergency." See Act of May 22, 1918, § 1(a), 40 Stat. 559; Act of June 21, 1941, ch. 210, § 1, 55 Stat. 252. When Congress enacted § 1182(f) in 1952, plaintiffs note, it borrowed "nearly verbatim" from those predecessor statutes, and one of the bill's sponsors affirmed that the provision would apply only during a time of crisis. According to plaintiffs, it therefore follows that Congress sought to delegate only a similarly tailored suspension power in § 1182(f). If anything, the drafting history suggests the opposite. In borrowing "nearly verbatim" from the pre-existing statute, Congress made one critical alteration—it removed the national emergency standard that plaintiffs now seek to reintroduce in another form.

Plaintiffs also strive to infer limitations from executive practice. By their count, every previous suspension order under § 1182(f) can be slotted into one of two categories. The vast majority targeted discrete groups of foreign nationals engaging in conduct "deemed harmful by the immigration laws." And the remaining entry restrictions that focused on entire nationalities—namely, President Carter's response to the Iran hostage crisis and President Reagan's suspension of immigration from Cuba—were, in their view, designed as a response to diplomatic emergencies "that the immigration laws do not address." Even if we were willing to confine expansive language in light of its past applications, the historical evidence is more equivocal than plaintiffs acknowledge. Presidents have repeatedly suspended entry not because the covered nationals themselves engaged in harmful acts but instead to retaliate for conduct by their governments that conflicted with U.S. foreign policy interests. See, e.g., Exec. Order No. 13662, 3 C.F.R. 233 (2014) (President Obama) (suspending entry of Russian nationals working in the financial services, energy, mining, engineering, or defense sectors, in light of the Russian Federation's "annexation of Crimea and its use of force in Ukraine"); Presidential Proclamation No. 6958, 3 C.F.R. 133 (1997) (President Clinton) (suspending entry of Sudanese governmental and military personnel, citing "foreign policy interests of the United States" based on Sudan's refusal to comply with United Nations resolution). And while some of these reprisals were directed at subsets of aliens from the countries at issue, others broadly suspended entry on the basis of nationality due to ongoing diplomatic disputes. . . .

Plaintiffs' final statutory argument is that the President's entry suspension violates § 1152(a)(1)(A), which provides that "no person shall . . . be discriminated against in the issuance of an immigrant visa because of the person's race, sex, nationality, place of birth, or place of residence." They contend that we should interpret the provision as prohibiting nationality-based discrimination throughout the entire immigration process. As an initial matter, this argument challenges only the validity of the entry restrictions on immigrant travel. Section 1152(a)(1)(A) is expressly limited to the issuance of "immigrant visa[s]" while § 1182(f) allows the President to suspend entry of "immigrants or nonimmigrants." [W]e reject plaintiffs' interpretation because it ignores the basic distinction between admissibility determinations and visa issuance that runs throughout the INA. . . .

Sections 1182(f) and 1152(a)(1)(A) thus operate in different spheres: Section 1182 defines the universe of aliens who are admissible into the United States (and therefore eligible to receive a visa). Once § 1182 sets the boundaries of admissibility into the United States, § 1152(a)(1)(A) prohibits discrimination in the allocation of immigrant visas based on nationality and other traits. The distinction between admissibility—to which § 1152(a)(1)(A) does not apply—and visa issuance—to which it does—is apparent from the text of the provision, which specifies only that its protections apply to the "issuance" of "immigrant visa[s]," without mentioning admissibility or entry. Had Congress instead intended in § 1152(a)(1)(A) to constrain the President's power to determine who may enter the country, it could easily have chosen language directed to that end. Section 1152(a)(1)(A) has never been treated as a constraint on the criteria for admissibility in § 1182. Presidents have repeatedly exercised their authority to suspend entry on the basis of nationality. As noted, President Reagan relied on § 1182(f) to suspend entry "as immigrants by all Cuban nationals," subject to exceptions. Proclamation No. 5517, 51 Fed. Reg. 30470 (1986). Likewise, President Carter invoked § 1185(a)(1) to deny and revoke visas to all Iranian nationals. On plaintiffs' reading, those orders were beyond the President's authority. The entry restrictions in the Proclamation on North Korea (which plaintiffs do not challenge in this litigation) would also be unlawful. Nor would the President be permitted to suspend entry from particular foreign states in response to an epidemic confined to a single region, or a verified terrorist threat involving nationals of a specific foreign nation, or even if the United States were on the brink of war. The text of § 1152(a)(1)(A) offers no standards that would enable courts to assess, for example, whether the situation in North Korea justifies entry restrictions while the terrorist threat in Yemen does not. The Proclamation is squarely within the scope of Presidential authority under the INA. Indeed, neither dissent even attempts any serious argument to the contrary, despite the fact that plaintiffs' primary contention below and in their briefing before this Court was that the Proclamation violated the statute.

IV

We now turn to plaintiffs' claim that the Proclamation was issued for the unconstitutional purpose of excluding Muslims. Because we have an obligation to assure ourselves of jurisdiction under Article III, we begin by addressing the question whether plaintiffs have standing to bring their constitutional challenge. . . .

In a case arising from an alleged violation of the Establishment Clause, a plaintiff must show, as in other cases, that he is "directly affected by the laws and practices against which [his] complaints are directed." *School Dist. of Abington Township v. Schempp*, 374 U.S. 203, 224, n. 9, 83 S.Ct. 1560, 10 L.Ed.2d 844 (1963). That is an issue here because the entry restrictions apply not to plaintiffs themselves but to others seeking to enter the United States.

Plaintiffs first argue that they have standing on the ground that the Proclamation "establishes a disfavored faith" and violates "their own right to be free from federal [religious] establishments." They describe such injury as "spiritual and dignitary."

We need not decide whether the claimed dignitary interest establishes an adequate ground for standing. The three individual plaintiffs assert another, more concrete injury: the alleged real-world effect that the Proclamation has had in keeping them separated from certain relatives who seek to enter the country. We agree that a person's interest in being united with his relatives is sufficiently concrete and particularized to form the basis of an Article III injury in fact. We therefore conclude that the individual plaintiffs have Article III standing to challenge the exclusion of their relatives under the Establishment Clause.

. . .Our cases recognize that "[t]he clearest command of the Establishment Clause is that one religious denomination cannot be officially preferred over another." *Larson v. Valente*, 456 U.S. 228, 244, 102 S.Ct. 1673, 72 L.Ed.2d 33 (1982). Plaintiffs believe that the Proclamation violates this prohibition by singling out Muslims for disfavored treatment. The entry suspension, they contend, operates as a "religious gerrymander," in part because most of the countries covered by the Proclamation have Muslim-majority populations. [P]laintiffs allege that the primary purpose of the Proclamation was religious animus and that the President's stated concerns about vetting protocols and national security were but pretexts for discriminating against Muslims. . . .

At the heart of plaintiffs' case is a series of statements by the President and his advisers casting doubt on the official objective of the Proclamation. For example, while a candidate on the campaign trail, the President published a "Statement on Preventing Muslim Immigration" that called for a "total and complete shutdown of Muslims entering the United States until our country's representatives can figure out what is going on." That statement remained on his campaign website until May 2017. Then-candidate Trump also stated that "Islam hates us" and asserted that the United States was "having problems with Muslims coming into the country." Shortly after being elected, when asked whether violence in Europe had affected his plans to "ban Muslim immigration," the President replied, "You know my plans. All along, I've been proven to be right." One week after his inauguration, the President issued EO-1. In a television interview, one of the President's campaign advisers explained that when the President "first announced it, he said, 'Muslim ban.' He called me up. He said, 'Put a commission together. Show me the right way to do it legally.'" The adviser said he assembled a group of Members of Congress and lawyers that "focused on, instead of religion, danger. . . . [The order] is based on places where there [is] substantial evidence that people are sending terrorists into our country." Plaintiffs also note that after issuing EO-2 to replace EO-1, the President expressed regret that his prior order had been "watered down" and called for a "much tougher version" of his "Travel Ban." Shortly before the release of the Proclamation, he stated that the "travel ban . . . should be far larger, tougher, and more specific," but "stupidly that would not be politically correct." More recently, on November 29, 2017, the President retweeted links to three anti-Muslim propaganda videos. In response to questions about those videos, the President's deputy press secretary denied that the President thinks Muslims are a threat to the United States, explaining that "the President has been talking about these security issues for years now, from the campaign trail to the White House" and "has addressed these issues with the travel order that he issued earlier this year and the companion proclamation."

The President of the United States possesses an extraordinary power to speak to his fellow citizens and on their behalf. Our Presidents have frequently used that power to espouse the principles of religious freedom and tolerance on which this Nation was founded. Yet it cannot be denied that the Federal Government and the Presidents who have carried its laws into effect have—from the Nation's earliest days—performed unevenly in living up to those inspiring words. But the issue before us is not whether to denounce the statements. It is instead the significance of those statements in reviewing a Presidential directive, neutral on its face, addressing a matter within the core of executive responsibility. In doing so, we must consider not only the statements of a particular President, but also the authority of the Presidency itself. The case before us differs in numerous respects from the conventional Establishment Clause claim. Unlike the typical suit involving religious displays or school prayer, plaintiffs seek to invalidate a national security directive regulating the entry of aliens abroad. Their claim accordingly raises a number of delicate issues regarding the scope of the constitutional right and the manner of proof. The Proclamation, moreover, is facially neutral toward religion. Plaintiffs therefore ask the Court to probe the sincerity of the stated justifications for the policy by reference to extrinsic statements—many of which were made before the President took the oath of office. These various aspects of plaintiffs' challenge inform our standard of review. . . .

Because decisions in these matters may implicate "relations with foreign powers," or involve "classifications defined in the light of changing political and economic circumstances," such judgments "are frequently of a character more appropriate to either the Legislature or the Executive." *Mathews v. Diaz,* 426 U.S. 67, 81, 96 S.Ct. 1883, 48 L.Ed.2d 478 (1976). Nonetheless, although foreign nationals seeking admission have no constitutional right to entry, this Court has engaged in a circumscribed judicial inquiry when the denial of a visa allegedly burdens the constitutional rights of a U.S. citizen. In *Kleindienst v. Mandel*, the Attorney General denied admission to a Belgian journalist and self-described "revolutionary Marxist," Ernest Mandel, who had been invited to speak at a conference at Stanford University. The professors who wished to hear Mandel speak challenged that decision under the First Amendment, and we acknowledged that their constitutional "right to receive information" was implicated. But we limited our review to whether the Executive gave a "facially legitimate and bona fide" reason for its action. Given the authority of the political branches over admission, we held that "when the Executive exercises this [delegated] power negatively on the basis of a facially legitimate and bona fide reason, the courts will neither look behind the exercise of that discretion, nor test it by balancing its justification" against the asserted constitutional interests of U.S. citizens. . . .

Mandel's narrow standard of review "has particular force" in admission and immigration cases that overlap with "the area of national security." *Kerry v. Din*, 576 U.S. at ___, 135 S.Ct., at 2140 (KENNEDY, J., concurring in judgment). For one, "[j]udicial inquiry into the national-security realm raises concerns for the separation of powers" by intruding on the President's constitutional responsibilities in the area of foreign affairs. *Ziglar v. Abbasi,* 582 U.S. ___, ___, 137 S.Ct. 1843, 1861, 198 L.Ed.2d 290 (2017) (internal quotation marks omitted). For another, "when it comes to collecting evidence and drawing inferences" on questions of national security, "the lack of competence on the part of the courts is marked." *Humanitarian Law Project,* 561 U.S., at 34, 130 S.Ct. 2705. A conventional application of *Mandel,* asking only whether the policy is facially legitimate and bona fide, would put an end to our review. But the Government has suggested that it may be appropriate here for the inquiry to extend beyond the facial neutrality of the order. For our purposes today, we assume that we may look behind the face of the Proclamation to the extent of applying rational basis review. That standard of review considers whether the entry policy is plausibly related to the Government's stated objective to protect the country and improve vetting processes.

Given the standard of review, it should come as no surprise that the Court hardly ever strikes down a policy as illegitimate under rational basis scrutiny. On the few occasions where we have done so, a common thread has been that the laws at issue lack any purpose other than a "bare . . . desire to harm a politically unpopular group." *Department of Agriculture v. Moreno,* 413 U.S. 528, 534, 93 S.Ct. 2821, 37 L.Ed.2d 782 (1973). . . . The Proclamation is expressly premised on legitimate purposes: preventing entry of nationals who cannot be adequately vetted and inducing other nations to improve their practices. The text says nothing about religion. Plaintiffs and the dissent nonetheless emphasize that five of the seven nations currently included in the Proclamation have Muslim-majority populations. Yet that fact alone does not support an inference of religious hostility, given that the policy covers just 8% of the world's Muslim population and is limited to countries that were previously designated by Congress or prior administrations as posing national security risks. The Proclamation, moreover, reflects the results of a worldwide review process undertaken by multiple Cabinet officials and their agencies. While we of course "do not defer to the Government's reading of the First Amendment," the Executive's evaluation of the underlying facts is entitled to appropriate weight, particularly in the context of litigation involving "sensitive and weighty interests of national security and foreign affairs." *Humanitarian Law Project*, 561 U.S., at 33–34, 130 S.Ct. 2705.

Three additional features of the entry policy support the Government's claim of a legitimate national security interest. First, since the President introduced entry restrictions in January 2017, three Muslim-majority countries—Iraq, Sudan, and Chad—have been removed from the list of covered countries. Second, for those countries that remain subject to entry restrictions, the Proclamation includes significant exceptions for various categories of foreign nationals. The policy permits nationals from nearly every covered country to travel to the United States on a variety of nonimmigrant visas. Third, the Proclamation creates a waiver program open to all covered foreign nationals seeking entry as immigrants or nonimmigrants. . . .

Finally, the dissent invokes *Korematsu v. United States*, 323 U.S. 214, 65 S.Ct. 193, 89 L.Ed. 194 (1944). Whatever rhetorical advantage the dissent may see in doing so, *Korematsu* has nothing to do with this case. The forcible relocation of U.S. citizens to concentration camps, solely and explicitly on the basis of race, is objectively unlawful and outside the scope of Presidential authority. But it is wholly inapt to liken that morally repugnant order to a facially neutral policy denying certain foreign nationals the privilege of admission. The entry suspension is an act that is well within executive authority and could have been taken by any other President—the only question is evaluating the actions of this particular President in promulgating an otherwise valid Proclamation.

The dissent's reference to *Korematsu*, however, affords this Court the opportunity to make express what is already obvious: *Korematsu* was gravely wrong the day it was decided, has been overruled in the court of history, and—to be clear—"has no place in law under the Constitution." 323 U.S., at 248, 65 S.Ct. 193 (Jackson, J., dissenting).

Because plaintiffs have not shown that they are likely to succeed on the merits of their claims, we reverse the grant of the preliminary injunction as an abuse of discretion. Our disposition of the case makes it unnecessary to consider the propriety of the nationwide scope of the injunction issued by the District Court.

The judgment of the Court of Appeals is reversed, and the case is remanded for further proceedings consistent with this opinion.

It is so ordered.

JUSTICE KENNEDY, concurring.

. . .[I]t is appropriate to make this further observation. There are numerous instances in which the statements and actions of Government officials are not subject to judicial scrutiny or intervention. That does not mean those officials are free to disregard the Constitution and the rights it proclaims and protects. The oath that all officials take to adhere to the Constitution is not confined to those spheres in which the Judiciary can correct or even comment upon what those officials say or do. Indeed, the very fact that an official may have broad discretion, discretion free from judicial scrutiny, makes it all the more imperative for him or her to adhere to the Constitution and to its meaning and its promise. An anxious world must know that our Government remains committed always to the liberties the Constitution seeks to preserve and protect, so that freedom extends outward, and lasts.

JUSTICE THOMAS, concurring.

. . .I write separately to address the remedy that the plaintiffs sought and obtained in this case. The District Court imposed an injunction that barred the Government from enforcing the President's Proclamation against anyone, not just the plaintiffs. Injunctions that prohibit the Executive Branch from applying a law or policy against anyone—often called "universal" or "nationwide" injunctions have become increasingly common. District courts, including the one here, have begun imposing universal injunctions without considering their authority to grant such sweeping relief. These injunctions are beginning to take a toll on the federal court system—preventing legal questions from percolating through the federal courts, encouraging forum shopping, and making every case a national emergency for the courts and for the Executive Branch. . . .

These injunctions are a recent development, emerging for the first time in the 1960s and dramatically increasing in popularity only very recently. And they appear to conflict with several traditional rules of equity, as well as the original understanding of the judicial role. No persuasive defense has yet been offered for the practice. Defenders of these injunctions contend that they ensure that individuals who did not challenge a law are treated the same as plaintiffs who did, and that universal injunctions give the judiciary a powerful tool to check the Executive Branch. But these arguments do not explain how these injunctions are consistent with the historical limits on equity and judicial power.

JUSTICE BREYER, with whom JUSTICE KAGAN joins, dissenting.

The question before us is whether Proclamation No. 9645 is lawful. If its promulgation or content was significantly affected by religious animus against Muslims, it would violate the relevant statute or the First Amendment itself. If, however, its sole *ratio decidendi* was one of national security, then it would be unlikely to violate either the statute or the Constitution. Which is it?

In my view, the Proclamation's elaborate system of exemptions and waivers can and should help us answer this question. [I]f the Government is applying the exemption and waiver provisions as written, then its argument for the Proclamation's lawfulness is strengthened. For one thing, the Proclamation then resembles more closely the two important Presidential precedents on point, President Carter's Iran order and President Reagan's Cuba proclamation, both of which contained similar categories of persons authorized to obtain case-by-case exemptions. Further, since the case-by-case exemptions and waivers apply without regard to the individual's religion, application of that system would help make clear that the Proclamation does not deny visas to numerous Muslim individuals (from those countries) who do not pose a security threat. And, perhaps most importantly, if the Government is not applying the Proclamation's exemption and waiver system, the claim that the Proclamation is a "Muslim ban," rather than a "security-based" ban, becomes much stronger. How could the Government successfully claim that the Proclamation rests on security needs if it is excluding Muslims who satisfy the Proclamation's own terms? At the same time, denying visas to Muslims who meet the Proclamation's own security terms would support the view that the Government excludes them for reasons based upon their religion.

Unfortunately there is evidence that supports the second possibility, i.e., that the Government is not applying the Proclamation as written. The Proclamation provides that the Secretary of State and the Secretary of Homeland Security "shall coordinate to adopt guidance" for consular officers to follow when deciding whether to grant a waiver. § 3(c)(ii). Yet, to my knowledge, no guidance has issued. . . . An examination of publicly available statistics also provides cause for concern. The State Department reported that during the Proclamation's first month, two waivers were approved out of 6,555 eligible applicants. *Amici* have suggested that there are numerous applicants who could meet the waiver criteria. For instance, the Proclamation anticipates waivers for those with "significant business or professional obligations" in the United States, § 3(c)(iv)(C), and amici identify many scholars who would seem to qualify. The Proclamation also anticipates waivers for those with a "close family member (e.g., a spouse, child, or parent)" in the United States, § 3(c)(iv)(D), and *amici* identify many such individuals affected by the Proclamation. Brief for Labor Organizations as *Amici Curiae* 15–18 (identifying children and other relatives of U.S. citizens).

Other data suggest the same. The Proclamation does not apply to asylum seekers or refugees. §§ 3(b)(vi), 6(e). Yet few refugees have been admitted since the Proclamation took effect. While more than 15,000 Syrian refugees arrived in the United States in 2016, only 13 have arrived since January 2018. Similarly few refugees have been admitted since January from Iran (3), Libya (1), Yemen (0), and Somalia (122). The Proclamation also exempts individuals applying for several types of nonimmigrant visas: lawful permanent residents, parolees, those with certain travel documents, dual nationals of noncovered countries, and representatives of governments or international organizations. §§ 3(b)(i)-(v). It places no restrictions on the vast majority of student and exchange visitors. In practice, however, only 258 student visas were issued to applicants from Iran (189), Libya (29), Yemen (40), and Somalia (0) in the first three months of 2018. This is less than a quarter of the volume needed to be on track for 2016 student visa levels. While this is but a piece of the picture, it does not provide grounds for confidence.

Anecdotal evidence further heightens these concerns. For example, one amicus identified a child with cerebral palsy in Yemen. The war had prevented her from receiving her medication, she could no longer move or speak, and her doctors said she would not survive in Yemen. Her visa application was denied. . . [I]n a pending case in the Eastern District of New York, a consular official has filed a sworn affidavit asserting that he and other officials do not, in fact, have discretion to grant waivers. According to the affidavit, consular officers "were not allowed to exercise that discretion" and "the waiver [process] is merely 'window dressing.' ". . .

Declarations, anecdotal evidence, facts, and numbers taken from *amicus* briefs are not judicial factfindings. The Government has not had an opportunity to respond, and a court has not had an opportunity to decide. But, given the importance of the decision in this case, the need for assurance that the Proclamation does not rest upon a "Muslim ban," and the assistance in deciding the issue that answers to the "exemption and waiver" questions may provide, I would send this case back to the District Court for further proceedings. And, I would leave the injunction in effect while the matter is litigated. Regardless, the Court's decision today leaves the District Court free to explore these issues on remand.

JUSTICE SOTOMAYOR, with whom JUSTICE GINSBURG joins, dissenting.

The United States of America is a Nation built upon the promise of religious liberty. Our Founders honored that core promise by embedding the principle of religious neutrality in the First Amendment. The Court's decision today fails to safeguard that fundamental principle. It leaves undisturbed a policy first advertised openly and unequivocally as a "total and complete shutdown of Muslims entering the United States" because the policy now masquerades behind a facade of national-security concerns. But this repackaging does little to cleanse Presidential Proclamation No. 9645 of the appearance of discrimination that the President's words have created. Based on the evidence in the record, a reasonable observer would conclude that the Proclamation was motivated by anti-Muslim animus. That alone suffices to show that plaintiffs are likely to succeed on the merits of their Establishment Clause claim. The majority holds otherwise by ignoring the facts, misconstruing our legal precedent, and turning a blind eye to the pain and suffering the Proclamation inflicts upon countless families and individuals, many of whom are United States citizens. Because that troubling result runs contrary to the Constitution and our precedent, I dissent.

. . .The Establishment Clause forbids government policies "respecting an establishment of religion." U.S. Const., Amdt. 1. The "clearest command" of the Establishment Clause is that the Government cannot favor or disfavor one religion over another. *Larson v. Valente*, 456 U.S. 228, 244, 102 S.Ct. 1673, 72 L.Ed.2d 33 (1982); *Church of Lukumi Babalu Aye, Inc. v. Hialeah*, 508 U.S. 520, 532, 113 S.Ct. 2217, 124 L.Ed.2d 472 (1993) ("[T]he First Amendment forbids an official purpose to disapprove of a particular religion"). That is so, this Court has held, because such acts send messages to members of minority faiths " 'that they are outsiders, not full members of the political community.' " *Santa Fe Independent School Dist. v. Doe*, 530 U.S. 290, 309, 120 S.Ct. 2266, 147 L.Ed.2d 295 (2000) To determine whether plaintiffs have proved an Establishment Clause violation, the Court asks whether a reasonable observer would view the government action as enacted for the purpose of disfavoring a religion. . . .

Although the majority briefly recounts a few of the statements and background events that form the basis of plaintiffs' constitutional challenge, that highly abridged account does not tell even half of the story. The full record paints a far more harrowing picture, from which a reasonable observer would readily conclude that the Proclamation was motivated by hostility and animus toward the Muslim faith.

During his Presidential campaign, then-candidate Donald Trump pledged that, if elected, he would ban Muslims from entering the United States. Specifically, on December 7, 2015, he issued a formal statement "calling for a total and complete shutdown of Muslims entering the United States. . . According to Pew Research, among others, there is great hatred towards Americans by large segments of the Muslim population." On December 8, 2015, Trump justified his proposal during a television interview by noting that President Franklin D. Roosevelt "did the same thing" with respect to the internment of Japanese Americans during World War II. A month later, at a rally in South Carolina, Trump told an apocryphal story about United States General John J. Pershing killing a large group of Muslim insurgents in the Philippines with bullets dipped in pigs' blood in the early 1900's. In March 2016, he expressed his belief that "Islam hates us. . . . [W]e can't allow people coming into this country who have this hatred of the United States . . . [a]nd of people that are not Muslim." That same month, Trump asserted that "[w]e're having problems with the Muslims, and we're having problems with Muslims coming into the country." He therefore called for surveillance of mosques in the United States, blaming terrorist attacks on Muslims' lack of "assimilation" and their commitment to "sharia law." A day later, he opined that Muslims "do not respect us at all" and "don't respect a lot of the things that are happening throughout not only our country, but they don't respect other things." In June 2016, he described the proposal as rooted in the need to stop "importing radical Islamic terrorism to the West through a failed immigration system." Asked in July 2016 whether he was "pull[ing] back from" his pledged Muslim ban, Trump responded, "I actually don't think it's a rollback. In fact, you could say it's an expansion." He then explained that he used different terminology because "[p]eople were so upset when [he] used the word Muslim." A month before the 2016 election, Trump reiterated that his proposed "Muslim ban" had "morphed into a[n] extreme vetting from certain areas of the world." Then, on December 21, 2016, President-elect Trump was asked whether he would "rethink" his previous "plans to create a Muslim registry or ban Muslim immigration." He replied: "You know my plans. All along, I've proven to be right." On January 27, 2017, one week after taking office, President Trump signed Executive Order EO-1, entitled "Protecting the Nation From Foreign Terrorist Entry Into the United States." As he signed it, President Trump read the title, looked up, and said "We all know what that means." That same day, President Trump explained to the media that, under EO-1, Christians would be given priority for entry as refugees into the United States. In particular, he bemoaned the fact that in the past, "[i]f you were a Muslim [refugee from Syria] you could come in, but if you were a Christian, it was almost impossible." The following day, one of President Trump's key advisers candidly drew the connection between EO-1 and the "Muslim ban" that the President had pledged to implement if elected. According to that adviser, "[W]hen [Donald Trump] first announced it, he said, 'Muslim ban.' He called me up. He said, 'Put a commission together. Show me the right way to do it legally.' ". . .

While litigation over EO-2 was ongoing, President Trump repeatedly made statements alluding to a desire to keep Muslims out of the country. For instance, he said at a rally of his supporters that EO-2 was just a "watered down version of the first one" and had been "tailor[ed]" at the behest of "the lawyers." He further added that he would prefer "to go back to the first [executive order] and go all the way" and reiterated his belief that it was "very hard" for Muslims to assimilate into Western culture. During a rally in April 2017, President Trump recited the lyrics to a song called "The Snake," a song about a woman who nurses a sick snake back to health but then is attacked by the snake, as a warning about Syrian refugees entering the country. And in June 2017, the President stated on Twitter that the Justice Department had submitted a "watered down, politically correct version" of the "original Travel Ban" "to S[upreme] C[ourt]." The President went on to tweet: "People, the lawyers and the courts can call it whatever they want, but I am calling it what we need and what it is, a TRAVEL BAN!" He added: "That's right, we need a TRAVEL BAN for certain DANGEROUS countries, not some politically correct term that won't help us protect our people!" In September 2017, President Trump tweeted that "[t]he travel ban into the United States should be far larger, tougher and more specific—but stupidly, that would not be politically correct!" On November 29, 2017, President Trump "retweeted" three anti-Muslim videos, entitled "Muslim Destroys a Statue of Virgin Mary!", "Islamist mob pushes teenage boy off roof and beats him to death!", and "Muslim migrant beats up Dutch boy on crutches!" Those videos were initially tweeted by a British political party whose mission is to oppose "all alien and destructive politic[al] or religious doctrines, including . . . Islam.". . .

Taking all the relevant evidence together, a reasonable observer would conclude that the Proclamation was driven primarily by anti-Muslim animus, rather than by the Government's asserted national-security justifications. Moreover, despite several opportunities to do so, President Trump has never disavowed any of his prior statements about Islam. Instead, he has continued to make remarks that a reasonable observer would view as an unrelenting attack on the Muslim religion and its followers. Notably, the Court recently found less pervasive official expressions of hostility and the failure to disavow them to be constitutionally significant. Cf. *Masterpiece Cakeshop, Ltd. v. Colorado Civil Rights Comm'n*, 584 U.S. ___, ___, 138 S.Ct. 1719, 1732, ___ L.Ed.2d ___ (2018) ("The official expressions of hostility to religion in some of the commissioners' comments—comments that were not disavowed at the Commission or by the State at any point in the proceedings that led to the affirmance of the order—were inconsistent with what the Free Exercise Clause requires"). It should find the same here. . . .

[T]he majority rightly declines to apply *Mandel*'s "narrow standard of review" and "assume[s] that we may look behind the face of the Proclamation." In doing so, however, the Court, without explanation or precedential support, limits its review of the Proclamation to rational-basis scrutiny. But even under rational-basis review, the Proclamation must fall. That is so because the Proclamation is " 'divorced from any factual context from which we could discern a relationship to legitimate state interests,' and 'its sheer breadth [is] so discontinuous with the reasons offered for it' " that the policy is " 'inexplicable by anything but animus.' " *Romer v. Evans*, 517 U.S. 620, 632, 635, 116 S.Ct. 1620, 134 L.Ed.2d 855 (1996); see also *Cleburne v. Cleburne Living Center, Inc.*, 473 U.S. 432, 448, 105 S.Ct. 3249, 87 L.Ed.2d 313 (1985) (recognizing that classifications predicated on discriminatory animus can never be legitimate because the Government has no legitimate interest in exploiting "mere negative attitudes, or fear" toward a disfavored group). [N]one of the features of the Proclamation highlighted by the majority supports the Government's claim that the Proclamation is genuinely and primarily rooted in a legitimate national-security interest. What the unrebutted evidence actually shows is that a reasonable observer would conclude, quite easily, that the primary purpose and function of the

Proclamation is to disfavor Islam by banning Muslims from entering our country. . . .

The First Amendment stands as a bulwark against official religious prejudice and embodies our Nation's deep commitment to religious plurality and tolerance. That constitutional promise is why, "[f]or centuries now, people have come to this country from every corner of the world to share in the blessing of religious freedom." *Town of Greece v. Galloway*, 572 U.S., at ___, 134 S.Ct., at 1841 (KAGAN, J., dissenting). Instead of vindicating those principles, today's decision tosses them aside. In holding that the First Amendment gives way to an executive policy that a reasonable observer would view as motivated by animus against Muslims, the majority opinion upends this Court's precedent, repeats tragic mistakes of the past, and denies countless individuals the fundamental right of religious liberty.

Just weeks ago, the Court rendered its decision in *Masterpiece Cakeshop*, 584 U.S. ___, 138 S.Ct. 1719, ___ L.Ed.2d ___, which applied the bedrock principles of religious neutrality and tolerance in considering a First Amendment challenge to government action. See id., at ___, 138 S.Ct., at 1731 ("The Constitution 'commits government itself to religious tolerance, and upon even slight suspicion that proposals for state intervention stem from animosity to religion or distrust of its practices, all officials must pause to remember their own high duty to the Constitution and to the rights it secures' " (quoting *Lukumi*, 508 U.S., at 547, 113 S.Ct. 2217)); *Masterpiece*, 584 U.S., at ___, 138 S.Ct., at 1732 (KAGAN, J., concurring) ("[S]tate actors cannot show hostility to religious views; rather, they must give those views 'neutral and respectful consideration' "). Those principles should apply equally here. In both instances, the question is whether a government actor exhibited tolerance and neutrality in reaching a decision that affects individuals' fundamental religious freedom. But unlike in *Masterpiece*, where a state civil rights commission was found to have acted without "the neutrality that the Free Exercise Clause requires," id., at ___, 138 S.Ct., at 1731, the government actors in this case will not be held accountable for breaching the First Amendment's guarantee of religious neutrality and tolerance. Unlike in *Masterpiece*, where the majority considered the state commissioners' statements about religion to be persuasive evidence of unconstitutional government action, id., at ___–___, 138 S.Ct., at 1728–1730, the majority here completely sets aside the President's charged statements about Muslims as irrelevant. That holding erodes the foundational principles of religious tolerance that the Court elsewhere has so emphatically protected, and it tells members of minority religions in our country " 'that they are outsiders, not full members of the political community.' " *Santa Fe*, 530 U.S., at 309, 120 S.Ct. 2266.

Today's holding is all the more troubling given the stark parallels between the reasoning of this case and that of *Korematsu v. United States*, 323 U.S. 214, 65 S.Ct. 193, 89 L.Ed. 194 (1944). Although a majority of the Court in *Korematsu* was willing to uphold the Government's actions based on a barren invocation of national security, dissenting Justices warned of that decision's harm to our constitutional fabric. Justice Murphy recognized that there is a need for great deference to the Executive Branch in the context of national security, but cautioned that "it is essential that there be definite limits to [the government's] discretion," as "[i]ndividuals must not be left impoverished of their constitutional rights on a plea of military necessity that has neither substance nor support." 323 U.S., at 234, 65 S.Ct. 193 (Murphy, J., dissenting). Justice Jackson lamented that the Court's decision upholding the Government's policy would prove to be "a far more subtle blow to liberty than the promulgation of the order itself," for although the executive order was not likely to be long lasting, the Court's willingness to tolerate it would endure.

In the intervening years since *Korematsu*, our Nation has done much to leave its sordid legacy behind. Today, the Court takes the important step of finally overruling *Korematsu,* denouncing it as "gravely wrong the day it was decided." This formal repudiation of a shameful precedent is laudable and long overdue. But it does not make the majority's decision here acceptable or right. By blindly accepting the Government's misguided invitation to sanction a discriminatory policy motivated by animosity toward a disfavored group, all in the name of a superficial claim of national security, the Court redeploys the same dangerous logic underlying *Korematsu* and merely replaces one "gravely wrong" decision with another.

Our Constitution demands, and our country deserves, a Judiciary willing to hold the coordinate branches to account when they defy our most sacred legal commitments. Because the Court's decision today has failed in that respect, with profound regret, I dissent.

NOTES

1. The majority cites *Kleindienst v. Mandel* for a "circumscribed judicial inquiry" to Executive Branch actions related to the exclusion of aliens ("whether the Executive gave a 'facially legitimate and bona fide' reason for its actions"). However, at the government's invitation, the majority did "look behind" President Trump's travel ban and considered his statements about Islam. Should the Court have adjusted its standard of review based on the government's concession? Will the government reconsider making such concessions in future cases? Does the *Mandel* framework apply to claims that the Executive Branch violated the Establishment Clause by acting pursuant to an unconstitutional purpose? Justice Sotomayor, who dissented, cited

Kerry v. Din, a recent application of *Mandel,* for the proposition that a facial review only applies absent evidence of "bad faith." Assuming that *Mandel* controls, what evidence, if any, would have triggered a more exacting review? The majority appears to acknowledge that the President's statements were discriminatory ("Plaintiffs argue that this President's words strike at fundamental standards of respect and tolerance, in violation of our constitutional tradition. But the issue before us is not whether to denounce the statements"). Moreover, the President revised his order twice. Did the President do this to make his order appear more acceptable? Did the third iteration "cure" any appearance of a bad motive from the prior orders? See *McCreary v. ACLU of Kentucky,* 545 U.S. 844, 866 n. 14 (2005). Given the Court's broad deference to the Executive's claim of national security, are there any circumstances in which the Court would override a president's claim? An *Amicus* brief by former national security officials argued that the government had "failed to come forward with information evincing a security need for its action" yet the majority did not question the legitimacy of the President's claim. Why? Does the Court assume that given the executive's superior knowledge about national security, the Court will not challenge the executive's assertions even when the executive's decisions are dubious? National security can be invoked to embrace domestic issues as well (President Trump invoked national security to justify expelling transgender people from the military). Will the Court defer in these instances as well?

2.   The majority acknowledges that *Korematsu v. United States,* which upheld the executive's internment of Japanese Americans in World War II as justified by national security concerns, was "gravely wrong the day it was decided," but "has nothing to do with the travel ban case." Justice Sotomayor disagreed, stating that the Court has "replaced one gravely wrong decision with another." Who is correct? Is *Korematsu* distinguishable from *Trump v. Hawaii?*

5–8   APPOINTMENT AND REMOVAL POWER

Unabridged, p. 489; add to end of *Notes,* new Note 9:

9.   OFFICERS OF THE UNITED STATES. *Lucia v. Securities and Exchange Commission,* 138 S.Ct. 2044, 201 L.Ed.2d 464 (2018). The Appointments Clause of the Constitution (Art. II, § 2, cl. 2) makes a distinction between "Officers of the United States" and mere employees of the federal government, and lays out the permissible methods of appointing these officers—either by the President, "Courts of Law," or "Heads of Departments." Raymond Lucia and his investment company were charged by the Securities and Exchange Commission (SEC) with violating the Investors Advisers Act by deceiving prospective clients on retirement savings accounts. The Commission delegated an administrative law judge (ALJ) to adjudicate Lucia's case. The Commission has five ALJs, all of whom were selected by staff members rather than the Commission proper, to adjudicate cases. ALJs assigned to hear enforcement actions have extensive powers, including

supervising discovery; issuing, revoking, or modifying subpoenas; deciding motions; ruling on the admissibility of evidence; administering oaths; hearing and examining witnesses; regulating the hearing and the conduct of parties and their counsel; and imposing sanctions for contemptuous conduct or violations of procedural rules. An SEC ALJ "exercises authority comparable to that of a federal district judge conducting a bench trial." After a hearing the ALJ makes findings and conclusions about the facts and law and issues an initial decision. The Commission can review that decision but if it chooses not to, the ALJ's decision becomes final and is deemed the action of the Commission.

After nine days of testimony the ALJ issued a decision concluding that Lucia had violated the Act and imposed sanctions, including civil penalties of $300,000 and a lifetime bar from the investment industry. On appeal to the SEC, Lucia claimed that the administrative proceeding was invalid because the ALJ was "an officer of the United States" and since he had not been constitutionally appointed, he lacked constitutional authority to do his job. The Commission rejected Lucia's argument because ALJs do not exercise "significant authority" and the D.C. Circuit sitting *en banc* upheld the Commission's order. Kagan, J., for the Court (7–2), reversed. The framework for distinguishing between "officers" and "employees" is laid out in *United States v. Germaine*, 99 U.S. 508 (1879) and *Buckley v. Valeo*, 424 U.S. 1 (1976). Under *Germaine,* an individual must occupy a "continuing position established by law" to qualify as an officer, rather than perform duties that are "occasional and temporary." Under *Buckley,* an individual must exercise "significant authority pursuant to the laws of the United States." This two-part framework was applied in *Freytag v. Commissioner,* 501 U.S. 868 (1991) to hold that special trial judges (STJs) of the United States Tax Court exercise significant authority in presiding over major tax disputes, and prepare findings and an opinion as a regular Tax Court judge. Even though the STJ could not enter a final decision, the Court held the STJs are "officers" because they hold a continuing office established by law and wield significant authority in presiding over adversarial hearings, conducting trials, and ruling on evidence and discovery. "*Freytag* says everything to decide this case." Indeed, given the fact that an ALJ decision can be final, whereas an STJ decision is not, an ALJ "can play the more autonomous role." "This is an *a fortiori* case: If the Tax Court's STJs are officers, as *Freytag* held, then the Commission's ALJs musty be too."

CHAPTER 6

DUE PROCESS

∎ ∎ ∎

6–3 THE NEW PROCEDURAL DUE PROCESS

6–3.2 DETERMINING WHAT PROCESS IS DUE

Unabridged, p. 577; add to end of *Notes*, new Note 6:

Abridged, p. 454; add to end of *Notes*, new Note 3:

Nelson v. Colorado, 581 U.S. ___, 137 S.Ct. 1249, 197 L.Ed.2d 611 (2017). In two separate cases, Colorado convicted Nelson and Madden of different crimes. The lower courts sentenced them to prison terms and payment of fees, court costs, and restitution. The state courts on appeal reversed their convictions. At retrial, Nelson was acquitted, and the state decided not to retry Madden. Each then sought the return of fees, court costs and restitution that they had paid to the state. The Colorado Supreme Court rejected their claims because the relevant state statute requires a claimant to prove by clear and convincing evidence that he or she innocent. The Supreme Court reversed (7 to 1), applying *Mathews v. Eldridge* (1976). The relevant factors are (1) the private interest affected, (2) the risk of an erroneous deprivation of that interest, and (3) the relevant governmental interests. All three factors weighed decisively against the Colorado procedure, which therefore was unconstitutional. "Colorado may not retain funds taken from Nelson and Madden solely because of their now-invalidated convictions, for Colorado may not presume a person, adjudged guilty of no crime, nonetheless guilty enough for monetary exactions."

6–5 IMPAIRMENT OF CONTRACTS

Unabridged, p. 596; add to end of *Notes,* new Note 4:

4. *Sveen v. Melin*, 138 S.Ct. 1815, 197 L.Ed.2d 180 (2018). After Mark Sveen and Kaye Melin married, Sveen purchased a life insurance policy naming Melin as the primary beneficiary and designating his two children by a former marriage as contingent beneficiaries. Sveen and Melin divorced, but the divorce decree made no mention of the insurance policy and Sveen took no action to revise his beneficiary designations. After Sveen died, Melin and Sveen's children made competing claims to the insurance proceeds. Sveen's children relied on a Minnesota statute passed after the Sveen-Melin marriage

but before the divorce which provided that "the dissolution or annulment of a marriage revokes any revocable beneficiary designation made by an individual to the individual's former spouse." The statute is based on the theory that the policyholder would want that result and if he does not, he could rename the ex-spouse as the beneficiary. The District Court, relying on the Minnesota revocation-on-divorce law, awarded the insurance proceeds to the children but the Eighth Circuit reversed, holding that the statute violates the Contracts Clause prohibition of a state "Impairing the Obligation of Contracts."

The Supreme Court, in an opinion by Kagan, J. (8–1), reversed, holding that the retroactive application of Minnesota's statute does not violate the Contracts Clause. The Court traced the history of laws governing revocation of wills and testamentary bequests, noting that the climbing divorce rates led almost all states to adopt revocation-on-divorce statutes which after a divorce automatically void testamentary bequests to a former spouse. Such laws rested on a judgment about the typical testator's probable intent, and that "the typical decedent would no more want his former spouse to benefit from his pension plan or life insurance than to inherit under his will." The decedent's failure to change the beneficiary "probably resulted from 'inattention' rather than 'intention.'"

The Contracts Clause restricts the power of states to "disrupt contractual arrangements," but "not all laws affecting pre-existing contracts violate the Clause." To determine whether a law crosses the constitutional line the Court has applied a two-step test: first, whether the state law has "substantially impaired" a contractual relationship and second, if a substantial impairment has been shown, the Court asks whether the state law is drawn in an "appropriate" and "reasonable" way to advance "a significant and legitimate public interest." *Energy Reserves Group, Inc. v. Kansas Power & Light Co.*, 459 U.S. 400, 411–412 (1983). To determine whether there has been a substantial impairment the Court considers the extent to which the law undermines the contractual bargain, interferes with a party's reasonable expectations, and prevents the party from reinstating or safeguarding his rights. The Court stopped after step one, concluding that the revocation-on-divorcer statute does not substantially impair pre-existing contractual arrangements. "The statute is designed to reflect a policyholder's intent—and so to support, rather than impair, the contractual scheme." Further, "the law is unlikely to disturb any policyholder's expectations because it does no more than a divorce court could always have done." And finally, "the statute supplies a mere default rule, which the policyholder can undo in a moment."

Gorsuch, J., in dissent, argued that the statute "cannot survive an encounter with even the breeziest of Contracts Clause tests." In his view there is no reasonable justification for this impairment in light of readily available alternatives. Although legislation could alter contracts prospectively, the original intent of the Clause was to categorically prohibit states from passing laws that retroactively impair contractual obligations.

Moreover, a test that requires courts to decide whether an impairment of a contract is "substantial" or "reasonable" or that serves a "significant and legitimate public purpose" injects too great an uncertainty into contracts. "How are the people to know today whether their lawful contracts will be enforced tomorrow, or instead undone by a legislative majority with different sympathies?" "Should we worry that a balancing test risks investing judges with discretion to choose which contracts to enforce—a discretion that might be exercised with an eye to the identity (and popularity) of the parties or contracts at hand?" Even if the present statute might not be invalid in all applications, "it cannot be applied to contracts formed before its enactment."

6–6   THE TAKING OF PROPERTY [UNABRIDGED]

6–5   THE TAKING OF PROPERTY [ABRIDGED]

6–6.1   TAKING BY POSSESSION [UNABRIDGED]

6–5.1   TAKING BY POSSESSION [ABRIDGED]

Unabridged, p. 603; add to end of *Notes*, new Note 5:

Abridged, p. 472; add to end of *Notes*, new Note 3:

TAKING PERSONAL PROPERTY. *Horne v. Department of Agriculture*, 576 U.S. ___, 135 S.Ct. 2419, 192 L.Ed.2d 388 (2015). The Agricultural Marketing Agreement Act of 1937 authorizes the Secretary of Agriculture to promulgate "marketing orders" to help maintain stable markets for particular agricultural products. The marketing order for raisins imposed a requirement that growers set aside a certain percentage of their crop for the Government, free of charge. The Government then may sell those raisins in noncompetitive markets, donate them, or dispose of them by other means. If the Government realizes any profits (after subtracting expenses from administering the program), it distributes the net proceeds to the raisin growers. In 2002–03, The Government required raisin growers to set aside 47% of their raisin crop under the reserve requirement. In 2003–04, it required 30%. Horne refused to set aside any raisins, arguing that the reserve requirement was an unconstitutional taking of property without just compensation. The Government fined the Hornes the fair market value of the raisins as well as additional civil penalties for their failure to obey the raisin marketing order.

The Ninth Circuit held that the reserve requirement did not violate the Fifth Amendment because personal property has less protection than real property and because the Hornes retained an interest in any net proceeds of the property. The Ninth Circuit also held that Horne could avoid relinquishing large percentages of their crop by "planting different crops." Roberts, C.J., for the Court (8 to 1) rejected both arguments and held that the Fifth Amendment applies to personal property as well as real property.

There is a classic "taking" when the Government "directly appropriates private property for its own use," whether it is real or personal property. "The Government has a categorical duty to pay just compensation when it takes your car, just as when it takes your home." The fact that Horne had a contingent interest in a portion of the raisins' value did not negate the Government's duty to pay just compensation for what it took.

The Court also rejected the Government's argument that the reserve requirement is not a taking because raisin growers "voluntarily choose" to participate in the raisin market. The Government cannot take a landlord's property just because the landlord could choose a different occupation. " 'Let them sell wine' is probably not much more comforting to the raisin growers than similar retorts have been to others throughout history." Selling in interstate commerce is "not a special governmental benefit that the Government may hold hostage, to be ransomed by the waiver of constitutional protection." The Government owes "just compensation" to Horne, measured by the market value of the property at the time of the taking. The Government fined the Hornes the fair market value of the raisins, and "it cannot now disavow that valuation." The Government also may not collect the associated civil penalty.

6–7   THE SECOND AMENDMENT [UNABRIDGED]

6–6   THE SECOND AMENDMENT [ABRIDGED]

Unabridged, p. 637; add to end of *Notes*, new Note 4:

Abridged, p. 499; add to end of *Notes*, new Note 3:

Caetano v. Massachusetts, 577 U.S. ___, 136 S.Ct. 1027, 194 L.Ed.2d 99 (2016)(per curiam). The Massachusetts Supreme Judicial Court upheld a state law prohibiting the possession of stun guns after considering "whether a stun gun is the type of weapon contemplated by Congress in 1789 as being protected by the Second Amendment." The unanimous Court reversed and held that the state court's opinion directly contradicted *District of Columbia v. Heller* (2008). "[T]he Second Amendment extends, prima facie, to all instruments that constitute bearable arms, even those that were not in existence at the time of the founding."

Alito, J., joined by Thomas, J., concurred in the judgment: The "pertinent Second Amendment inquiry is whether stun guns are commonly possessed by law-abiding citizens for lawful purposes *today*." Only seven states ban stun guns. Caetano's abusive ex-boyfriend earlier put her in the hospital and ignored multiple restraining orders. A friend gave her a stun gun. When the ex-boyfriend threatened her after she left work, she displayed the stun gun and threatened to use it unless he left. "Massachusetts was either unable or unwilling to do what was necessary to protect her." Instead, "the

Commonwealth chose to deploy its prosecutorial resources to prosecute and convict her of a criminal offense for arming herself with a nonlethal weapon that may well have saved her life."

Later that same term, the Court decided, *Voisine v. United States*, 579 U.S. ___, 136 S.Ct. 2272, 195 L.Ed.2d 736 (2016)(6 to 2). Federal law prohibits any person convicted of a "misdemeanor crime of domestic violence" from possessing a firearm. 18 U.S.C. § 922(g)(9). The statute defines that to include any misdemeanor committed against a domestic relation that necessarily involves the "use . . . of physical force." The Court held (6 to 2) that a misdemeanor assault conviction for reckless (as contrasted to knowing or intentional) conduct triggers the statutory firearms ban. Kagan, J., spoke for the Court. Recklessness "is the result of a deliberate decision to endanger another." The relevant term, "use," is "indifferent as to whether the actor has the mental state of intention, knowledge, or recklessness with respect to the harmful consequences of his volitional conduct." Congress enacted § 922(g)(9) "in order to prohibit domestic abusers convicted under run-of-the-mill misdemeanor assault and battery laws from possessing guns." Most states allow recklessness to prove assault.

Thomas, J., joined by Sotomayor, J., dissented on statutory interpretation grounds. In the portion of the dissent Sotomayor did not join, Thomas also argued that the majority read "the statute in a way that creates serious constitutional problems." The way the Court reads the statute, a "mother who slaps her 18-year-old son for talking back to her—an intentional use of force—could lose her right to bear arms forever if she is cited by the police under a local ordinance. The majority seeks to expand that already broad rule to any reckless physical injury or nonconsensual touch. I would not extend the statute into that constitutionally problematic territory."

CHAPTER 7

STATE ACTION

• • •

7–5 LICENSING

Unabridged, p. 678; after Jackson v. Metropolitan Edison Co., add the following:

Abridged, p. 427; after Jackson v. Metropolitan Edison Co., add the following:

NOTES

Manhattan Community Access Corp. v. Halleck, 139 S.Ct. 1921, ___ L.Ed.2d ___ (2019). The Cable Communications Policy Act of 1984 authorizes state and local governments to require cable TV operators to set aside channels for public access. The New York State Public Service Commission, which regulates cable franchising, authorizes municipalities to grant cable franchises to cable companies if the company agrees to set aside channels for public access. The channels must be operated free of charge on a first-come, first-served, nondiscriminatory basis. Time Warner, which operates the cable system in Manhattan, leased the operation of public access channels to Manhattan Community Access Corp. (MNN), an independent nonprofit corporation chosen by Manhattan's borough president. Respondents, film producers, produced a film shown on one of the public access channels that criticized MNN's neglect of the East Harlem community. As a result of the production, MNN suspended the respondents from using MNN facilities. Respondents sued, claiming that MNN violated their First Amendment right of free speech by restricting their access to the public channels because of the content of their film. The district court dismissed their suit, but the Second Circuit reversed, finding that the public access channels are a public forum for purposes of the First Amendment and that "New York City delegated to MNN the traditionally public function of administering speech in the public forum of Manhattan's public access channels."

The Supreme Court reversed (5–4) in an opinion by Kavanaugh, J. The Court held that MNN is a private entity, not a state actor, and therefore is not subject to Constitutional constraints. Under the state action doctrine, a private entity may be considered a state actor when it exercises a function "traditionally reserved to the state." *Jackson v. Metropolitan Edison Co.* However, the operation of a public access channel is not a traditional and exclusive public function. The Court observed that "very few" functions fall into the public function category, notably running elections and operating a company town. By contrast, operating public access channels has not traditionally and exclusively been performed by government. Nor can the producers be seen as operating a public forum for speech. Private entities often provide forums for speech, but that activity does not transform the private entity into a state actor. "If the rule were otherwise, all private property owners and private lessees who open their property for speech would be subject to First Amendment constraints." The fact that New York State heavily regulates MNN, and the City has designated MNN to operate the channels, does not make MNN a state actor. To be sure, the City could operate the channels itself, which would require the City to observe First Amendment constraints. But the City does not own or lease the channels, or possess a formal easement or other property interest in the channels. "The state-action doctrine enforces a critical boundary between government and the individual, and thereby protects a robust sphere of individual liberty. Expanding the state-action doctrine beyond its traditional boundaries would expand governmental control while restricting individual liberty and business enterprise. We decline to do so in this case."

Justice Sotomayor, joined by Ginsburg, Breyer, and Kagan JJ., dissented. "This case is not about a private property owner that simply opened up its property to others." New York City secured a property interest in public access TV channels when it granted a license to a cable company and regulated the manner in which the company administered the channels on terms that made the public access channels a public forum. Just as the city would be subject to the First Amendment had it chosen to run the forum itself, the City opened up the setting for speech when it delegated control and administration of the forum to MNN, which assumed the same responsibility as the City when it accepted the delegation. To be sure, the Court has not defined precisely what kind of government property interest is necessary for a public forum to exist. The dissent noted that the Court had previously stated that a public forum might be created when "a speaker seeks access to public property or to private property dedicated to public use.," *Cornelius v. NAACP Legal Defense & Ed. Fund, Inc.,* 473 U.S. 788, 801 (1985), but the majority dismissed the reference in *Cornelius* as "passing dicta." The dissent further argued that the government's property interest in this case is akin to an easement. If the cable wires were a road, or a theater, there would be no question that the government's long-term lease to a private entity would be sufficient for a public forum to exist. Just as a doctor who is hired by a prison to provide medical care to state prisoners is a state actor for purposes of a § 1983 lawsuit, see *West v. Atkins,* 487 U.S. 42 (1988), so is the City when it contracted out its constitutional responsibilities to a private entity. Otherwise, states would be free to outsource all of its services and leave its citizens with no means of redress. Nor is this a case in which a private entity enters the marketplace and is then subject to government regulation, as in *Jackson v. Metropolitan Edison Co.* MNN is not a private entity that simply ventured into the marketplace. It was asked to do so by the City which secured the public access channels, opened them up for public use as required by the State, and then deputized MNN to administer the channels. Just as a state has no constitutional obligation to operate prisons, the City has no constitutional obligation to operate public access channels. But once the City undertakes that responsibility, it must do so consistent with constitutional rules.

CHAPTER 8

EQUAL PROTECTION

∎ ∎ ∎

8–2 SUSPECT CLASSES AND OTHER CLASSIFICATIONS

8–2.1 RACE

8–2.14 Reverse Discrimination

8–2.14.1 Education

Unabridged, p. 770; add to end of *Notes*, to Note 6:

Abridged, p. 602; add to end of *Notes*, new Note 6:

Fisher v. University of Texas, 579 U.S. ___, 136 S.Ct. 2198, 195 L.Ed.2d 511 (2016)(4–3; Kagan, J., not participating). Kennedy, J., spoke for the Court. Plaintiff sued, claiming that the University of Texas' "consideration of race as part of its holistic-review process disadvantaged her and other Caucasian applicants in violation of the Equal Protection Clause." The University, following state law, offers to admit any student who graduates in the top 10% of a Texas high school. The University fills up the remaining spaces (about 25%) using a holistic review by counting various factors including race. It added this holistic review in response to *Gutter* in an effort to admit more minority students than the top 10% plan admitted.

The Court approved this holistic admission, although it wrote the opinion narrowly. "The University's program is *sui generis*." Fisher did not challenge the top 10% plan which "has been taken, somewhat artificially, as a given premise." Her decision not to challenge the top 10% plan "has led to a record that is almost devoid of information about the students who secured admission to the University through the Plan." Rather "than prolong a suit that has already persisted for eight years," the Court affirmed the lower court. "The fact that this case has been litigated on a somewhat artificial basis, furthermore, may limit its value for prospective guidance." In addition, the University has a "continuing obligation to satisfy the burden of strict scrutiny in light of changing circumstances." In 2003, at the time of *Gutter*, 11% of Texas residents enrolled in the University were Hispanic and 3.5% were black; in 2007, 16.9% of the freshmen were Hispanic and 6.8% were black. The increases "show that consideration of race has had a meaningful, if still limited, effect on the diversity of the University's freshman class."

Kennedy concluded by saying: "The Court's affirmance of the University's admissions policy today does not necessarily mean the University may rely on that same policy without refinement. It is the University's ongoing obligation to engage in constant deliberation and continued reflection regarding its admissions policies."

Alito, J., joined by Roberts, C.J., & Thomas, J., dissented. "[T]he majority notes that this litigation has persisted for many years, that petitioner has already graduated from another college, that UT's [University of Texas] policy may have changed over time, and that this case may offer little prospective guidance. At most, these considerations counsel in favor of dismissing this case as improvidently granted. . . . The majority cannot side with UT simply because it is tired of this case."

UT's consideration of race "pervades every aspect of UT's admissions process. See App. 219a ('We are certainly aware of the applicant's race. It's on the front page of the application that's being read [and] is used in context with everything else that's part of the applicant's file'). This is by design, as UT considers its use of racial classifications to be a benign form of 'social engineering.'" (Quoting Bill Powers, President of UT from 2006–2015). Alito also objected that UT provides no definition of the various ethnic groups. It "relies on applicants to 'classify themselves.' This is an invitation for applicants to game the system."

Alito added that UT admitted that "the [top 10%] percentage plan certainly helps with minority admissions, by and large," but UT argued it also needed its holistic review because it "needs race-conscious admissions in order to admit '[t]he African-American or Hispanic child of successful professionals in Dallas." "Thus, the Top Ten Percent Law is faulted for admitting *the wrong kind of African-American and Hispanic students.*" [Emphasis in original.] UT argues "it needs affirmative action to admit privileged minorities."

Thomas, J., also dissented: "[T]he Court's decision today is irreconcilable with strict scrutiny, rests on pernicious assumptions about race, and departs from many of our precedents."

8–3   FUNDAMENTAL RIGHTS

8–3.2   VOTING [UNABRIDGED]

8–3.1   VOTING [ABRIDGED]

8–3.21   Apportionment [Unabridged]

8–3.11   Apportionment [Abridged]

Unabridged, p. 853; add to end of *Notes*, new Note 7:

Abridged, p. 665; add to end of *Notes*, new Note 5:

Evenwel v. Abbott, 588 U.S. ___, 136 S.Ct. 1120, 194 L.Ed.2d 291 (2016). Texas draws its legislative districts on the basis of total population, for one person, one vote. The maximum total-population deviation of the state senate districts was 8.04%, well within the presumptively permissible 10% range. However, if one looked at eligible-voter or registered-voter population, the map's maximum population deviation exceeds 40% because some areas had a disproportionate number of nonvoters, such as aliens. Plaintiffs argued that basing apportionment on total population dilutes their votes in relation to voters in other Senate districts, in violation of one person, one vote. Ginsburg, J., for the Court (with no dissents), rejected this argument: "We hold, based on constitutional history, this Court's decisions, and longstanding practice, that a State *may draw* its legislative districts based on total population." (Emphasis added.) The Court acknowledged that two state constitutions authorize the exclusion of noncitizen immigrants, and a few states exclude certain non-permanent residents, including nonresident members of the military. Still, "Adopting voter-eligible apportionment as constitutional command would upset a well-functioning approach to districting that all 50 States and countless local jurisdictions have followed for decades, even centuries." The Court added, "we need not and do not resolve whether, as Texas now argues, States may draw district to equalize voter-eligible population rather than total population."

Thomas, J., and Alito, J., each filed opinions concurring in the judgment. In part of the Alito opinion (which Thomas joined), Alito made clear that he rejected the Solicitor General's argument that states *must* use total population because the Constitution allocates House seats based on total population. "[E]ven the allocation of House seats does not comport with one person, one vote," because each state is entitled to at least one representative. One Representative in Wyoming represents fewer than 570,000 people while the one next door in Montana represents nearly a million. Alito concludes, this case only holds that "Texas permissibly used total population in drawing the challenged legislative districts."

8–3.4   PRIVACY AND SEXUAL AUTONOMY [UNABRIDGED]

8–3.3   PRIVACY AND SEXUAL AUTONOMY [ABRIDGED]

8–3.43   Abortion [Unabridged]

8–3.33   Abortion [Abridged]

Unabridged, p. 935; add to end of *Notes*, new Note 4:

Abridged, p. 728; add to end of *Notes*, new Note 4:

    4.   *Whole Woman's Health v. Hellerstedt*, 579 U.S. ___, 136 S.Ct. 2293, 195 L.Ed.2d 665 (2016). Abortion providers sued Texas officials to enjoin them from implementing a statute (H.B. 2) that required abortion providers (1) to have admitting privileges at a local hospital located no more than 30 miles from their abortion facility and (2) to require that abortion facilities meet minimum standards in Texas for ambulatory surgical centers (ASCs). The trial court enjoined the law, but the Fifth Circuit reversed. The Supreme Court (5 to 3) reversed the Fifth Circuit and enjoined the law.

    Breyer, J., for the Court, first rejected the procedural obstacles to the plaintiffs' case. Res judicata does not bar plaintiffs, even though many of the same plaintiffs earlier lost a lawsuit seeking to invalidate this same Texas law. In the earlier case involving the admitting privileges prong of H.B.2, "plaintiffs brought their facial challenge to the admitting-privileges requirement *prior to its enforcement*—before many abortion clinics had closed and while it was still unclear how many clinics would be affected. Here, petitioners bring an as-applied challenge to the requirement *after its enforcement*—and after a large number of clinics have in fact closed. The post enforcement consequences of H.B. 2 were unknowable before it went into effect." (Emphasis in original.) New evidence can give rise to a new claim.

    In addition, there is no res judicata or issue preclusion to bar the challenge to the surgical care requirement because the plaintiffs in the earlier decision did not bring that claim, which is a separate and distinct provision of H.B. 2. Also, when the plaintiffs brought the earlier claim, the relevant Texas agency "had not yet issued" implementing regulations. "Finally, the relevant factual circumstances changed" since the earlier lower court decision.

    The Court went on to hold that both provisions impose an "undue burden" on women seeking abortion. First, complications requiring hospital admissions occur in less than one-half of 1% of the cases. Once the hospital admitting requirement went into effect, the number of abortion facilities "dropped in half, from 40 to about 20," and the "number of women of reproductive age living more than 50 miles from a clinic has doubled . . ." The surgical center requirement is also an undue burden. The trial court found that "risks are not appreciably lowered for patients who undergo abortions at ambulatory surgical centers as compared to nonsurgical-center facilities." Moreover, "the parties stipulated that the [ASC] requirement would further reduce the number of abortion facilities available to seven or eight facilities, located in Houston, Austin, San Antonio, and Dallas/Fort Worth." The Court concluded, "neither of these provisions confers medical benefits sufficient to justify the burdens upon access that each imposes. Each places a substantial obstacle in the path of women seeking a previability abortion, each constitutes an undue burden on abortion access, and each violates the Federal Constitution."

The Court said it was significant that "the relevant statute here does not set forth any legislative findings." Consequently, in examining the health benefits, it was proper for the district court, in the course of invalidating H.B. 2, to consider "the evidence in the record—including expert evidence, presented in stipulations, depositions, and testimony. It then weighed the asserted benefits against the burdens," and found that H.B. 2 imposed an undue burden.

The Court invalidated all of H.B. 2. It acknowledged, "The severability clause says that 'every provision, section, subsection, sentence, clause, phrase, or word in this Act, and every application of the provision in this Act, are severable from each other." Nonetheless, Breyer, for the Court, held that statute is not severable: "The provisions are unconstitutional on their face: Including a severability provision in the law does not change that conclusion." If such "a severability clause could impose such a [severability] requirement on courts, legislatures would easily be able to insulate unconstitutional statutes from most facial review."

Alito, J., joined by Roberts, C.J. & Thomas, J., dissented. He first focused on res judicata and issue preclusion:

> "[T]he Court's holding that petitioners' second facial challenge to the admitting privileges requirement is not barred by claim preclusion is not supported by any of our cases or any body of lower court precedent; is contrary to the bedrock rule that a party cannot relitigate a claim simply because the party has obtained new and better evidence; . . . In a regular case, an attempt by petitioners to relitigate their previously unsuccessful facial challenge to the admitting privileges requirement would have been rejected out of hand—indeed, might have resulted in the imposition of sanctions under Federal Rule of Civil Procedure 11. No court would even think of reviving such a claim on its own. But in this abortion case, ordinary rules of law—and fairness—are suspended."

On the merits, Alito said that the Court's conclusion that this law caused some abortion clinics to close "is belied by petitioners' own submissions to this Court." Petitioners "put on evidence of actual clinic capacity in their earlier case, and there is no apparent reason why they could not have done the same here." Instead, they just inferred that clinics closed because of H.B. 2.

H.B. 2 did cause *some* abortion clinics to close. After all, "H.B. 2 was intended to force unsafe facilities to shut down." Texas and other states enacted these restrictions "in the wake of the Kermit Gosnell scandal, in which a physician who ran an abortion clinic in Philadelphia was convicted for the first-degree murder of three infants who were born alive and for the manslaughter of a patient. Gosnell had not been actively supervised by state or local authorities or by his peers, and the Philadelphia grand jury that investigated the case recommended that the Commonwealth adopt a law requiring abortion clinics to comply with the same regulations as ASCs. If Pennsylvania had had such a requirement in force, the Gosnell facility may have been shut down before his crimes. And if there were any similarly unsafe facilities in Texas, H.B. 2 was clearly intended to put them out of business."

In answer to this argument, Breyer responded:

"Gosnell, a physician in Pennsylvania, was convicted of first-degree murder and manslaughter. He 'staffed his facility with unlicensed and indifferent workers, and then let them practice medicine unsupervised' and had '[d]irty facilities; unsanitary instruments; an absence of functioning monitoring and resuscitation equipment; the use of cheap, but dangerous, drugs; illegal procedures; and inadequate emergency access for when things inevitably went wrong.' Gosnell's behavior was terribly wrong. But there is no reason to believe that an extra layer of regulation would have affected that behavior. Determined wrongdoers, already ignoring existing statutes and safety measures, are unlikely to be convinced to adopt safe practices by a new overlay of regulations. Regardless, Gosnell's deplorable crimes could escape detection only because his facility went uninspected for more than 15 years."

Alito also objected to Breyer's severability argument:

"By forgoing severability, the Court strikes down numerous provisions that could not plausibly impose an undue burden. For example, surgical center patients must 'be treated with respect, consideration, and dignity.' That's now enjoined. Patients may not be given misleading 'advertising regarding the competence and/or capabilities of the organization.' Enjoined. Centers must maintain fire alarm and emergency communications systems, and eliminate '[h]azards that might lead to slipping, falling, electrical shock, burns, poisoning, or other trauma.' Enjoined and enjoined."

Thomas, J., also filed a separate dissent to "to emphasize how today's decision perpetuates the Court's habit of applying different rules to different constitutional rights—especially the putative right to abortion."

8–3.44   Homosexuality [Unabridged]

8–3.34   Homosexuality [Abridged]

Unabridged, p. 959; add to end of section:

Abridged, p. 751; add to end of section:

OBERGEFELL V. HODGES

576 U.S. ___, 135 S.Ct. 2584, 192 L.Ed.2d 609 (2015).

JUSTICE KENNEDY delivered the opinion of the Court.

The Constitution promises liberty to all within its reach, a liberty that includes certain specific rights that allow persons, within a lawful realm, to define and express their identity. The petitioners in these cases seek to find that liberty by marrying someone of the same sex and having their marriages deemed lawful on the same terms and conditions as marriages between persons of the opposite sex.

These cases come from Michigan, Kentucky, Ohio, and Tennessee, States that define marriage as a union between one man and one woman. . . . The Court of Appeals held that a State has no constitutional obligation to license same-sex marriages or to recognize same-sex marriages performed out of State. . . . This Court granted review, limited to two questions. The first, presented by the cases from Michigan and Kentucky, is whether the Fourteenth Amendment requires a State to license a marriage between two people of the same sex. The second, presented by the cases from Ohio, Tennessee, and, again, Kentucky, is whether the Fourteenth Amendment requires a State to recognize a same-sex marriage licensed and performed in a State which does grant that right. . . .

From their beginning to their most recent page, the annals of human history reveal the transcendent importance of marriage. The lifelong union of a man and a woman always has promised nobility and dignity to all persons, without regard to their station in life. Marriage is sacred to those who live by their religions and offers unique fulfillment to those who find meaning in the secular realm. . . .

The centrality of marriage to the human condition makes it unsurprising that the institution has existed for millennia and across civilizations. Since the dawn of history, marriage has transformed strangers into relatives, binding families and societies together. Confucius taught that marriage lies at the foundation of government. This wisdom was echoed centuries later and half a world away by Cicero, who wrote, "The first bond of society is marriage; next, children; and then the family." There are untold references to the beauty of marriage in religious and philosophical texts spanning time, cultures, and faiths, as well as in art and literature in all their forms. It is fair and necessary to say these references were based on the understanding that marriage is a union between two persons of the opposite sex.

That history is the beginning of these cases. The respondents say it should be the end as well. To them, it would demean a timeless institution if the concept and lawful status of marriage were extended to two persons of the same sex. Marriage, in their view, is by its nature a gender-differentiated union of man and woman. This view long has been held—and continues to be held—in good faith by reasonable and sincere people here and throughout the world.

The petitioners acknowledge this history but contend that these cases cannot end there. . . . Far from seeking to devalue marriage, the petitioners seek it for themselves because of their respect—and need—for its privileges and responsibilities. And their immutable nature dictates that same-sex marriage is their only real path to this profound commitment. . . .

The ancient origins of marriage confirm its centrality, but it has not stood in isolation from developments in law and society. The history of marriage is one of both continuity and change. That institution—even as confined to opposite-sex relations—has evolved over time. . . .

This Court first gave detailed consideration to the legal status of homosexuals in *Bowers* v. *Hardwick*, 478 U.S. 186 (1986). There it upheld the constitutionality of a Georgia law deemed to criminalize certain homosexual acts. Ten years later, in *Romer* v. *Evans*, 517 U.S. 620 (1996), the Court invalidated an amendment to Colorado's Constitution that sought to foreclose any branch or political subdivision of the State from protecting persons against discrimination based on sexual orientation. Then, in 2003, the Court overruled *Bowers*, holding that laws making same-sex intimacy a crime "demea[n] the lives of homosexual persons." *Lawrence* v. *Texas*, 539 U.S. 558, 575. . . .

The nature of injustice is that we may not always see it in our own times. The generations that wrote and ratified the Bill of Rights and the Fourteenth Amendment did not presume to know the extent of freedom in all of its dimensions, and so they entrusted to future generations a charter protecting the right of all persons to enjoy liberty as we learn its meaning. When new insight reveals discord between the Constitution's central protections and a received legal stricture, a claim to liberty must be addressed.

Applying these established tenets, the Court has long held the right to marry is protected by the Constitution. In *Loving* v. *Virginia*, 388 U.S. 1, 12 (1967), which invalidated bans on interracial unions, a unanimous Court held marriage is "one of the vital personal rights essential to the orderly pursuit of happiness by free men." The Court reaffirmed that holding in *Zablocki* v. *Redhail*, 434 U.S. 374, 384 (1978), which held the right to marry was burdened by a law prohibiting fathers who were behind on child support from marrying. The Court again applied this principle in *Turner* v. *Safley*, 482 U.S. 78, 95 (1987), which held the right to marry was abridged by regulations limiting the privilege of prison inmates to marry. Over time and in other contexts, the Court has reiterated that the right to marry is fundamental under the Due Process Clause. *Griswold, supra, Skinner* v. *Oklahoma ex rel. Williamson*, 316 U.S. 535, 541 (1942).

[T]his Court's cases describing the right to marry presumed a relationship involving opposite-sex partners. The Court, like many institutions, has made assumptions defined by the world and time of which it is a part. This was evident in *Baker* v. *Nelson*, 409 U.S. 810, a one-line summary decision issued in 1972, holding the exclusion of same-sex couples from marriage did not present a substantial federal question.

Still, there are other, more instructive precedents. This Court's cases have expressed constitutional principles of broader reach. In defining the right to marry these cases have identified essential attributes of that right based in history, tradition, and other constitutional liberties inherent in this intimate bond. [I]n assessing whether the force and rationale of its cases apply to same-sex couples, the Court must respect the basic reasons why the right to marry has been long protected.

This analysis compels the conclusion that same-sex couples may exercise the right to marry. The four principles and traditions to be discussed demonstrate that the reasons marriage is fundamental under the Constitution apply with equal force to same-sex couples.

A first premise of the Court's relevant precedents is that the right to personal choice regarding marriage is inherent in the concept of individual autonomy. This abiding connection between marriage and liberty is why *Loving* invalidated interracial marriage bans under the Due Process Clause. . . . The nature of marriage is that, through its enduring bond, two persons together can find other freedoms, such as expression, intimacy, and spirituality. . . .

A second principle in this Court's jurisprudence is that the right to marry is fundamental because it supports a two-person union unlike any other in its importance to the committed individuals. This point was central to *Griswold* v. *Connecticut*, which held the Constitution protects the right of married couples to use contraception. . . .

A third basis for protecting the right to marry is that it safeguards children and families and thus draws meaning from related rights of childrearing, procreation, and education. [M]any same-sex couples provide loving and nurturing homes to their children, whether biological or adopted. . . . Excluding same-sex couples from marriage thus conflicts with a central premise of the right to marry. Without the recognition, stability, and predictability marriage offers, their children suffer the stigma of knowing their families are somehow lesser. They also suffer the significant material costs of being raised by unmarried parents, relegated through no fault of their own to a more difficult and uncertain family life. The marriage laws at issue here thus harm and humiliate the children of same-sex couples.

That is not to say the right to marry is less meaningful for those who do not or cannot have children. An ability, desire, or promise to procreate is not and has not been a prerequisite for a valid marriage in any State. In light of precedent protecting the right of a married couple not to procreate, it cannot be said the Court or the States have conditioned the right to marry on the capacity or commitment to procreate. The constitutional marriage right has many aspects, of which childbearing is only one.

Fourth and finally, this Court's cases and the Nation's traditions make clear that marriage is a keystone of our social order. [J]ust as a couple vows to support each other, so does society pledge to support the couple, offering symbolic recognition and material benefits to protect and nourish the union. Indeed, while the States are in general free to vary the benefits they confer on all married couples, they have throughout our history made marriage the basis for an expanding list of governmental rights, benefits, and responsibilities. These aspects of marital status include: taxation; inheritance and property rights; rules of intestate succession; spousal privilege in the law of evidence; hospital access; medical decision making authority; adoption rights; the rights and benefits of survivors; birth and death certificates; professional ethics rules; campaign finance restrictions; workers' compensation benefits; health insurance; and child custody, support, and visitation rules. [B]y virtue of their exclusion from that institution, same-sex couples are denied the constellation of benefits that the States have linked to marriage. This harm results in more than just material burdens. . . . It demeans gays and lesbians for the State to lock them out of a central institution of the Nation's society. Same-sex couples, too, may aspire to the transcendent purposes of marriage and seek fulfillment in its highest meaning.

The limitation of marriage to opposite-sex couples may long have seemed natural and just, but its inconsistency with the central meaning of the fundamental right to marry is now manifest. With that knowledge must come the recognition that laws excluding same-sex couples from the marriage right impose stigma and injury of the kind prohibited by our basic charter.

. . . Many who deem same-sex marriage to be wrong reach that conclusion based on decent and honorable religious or philosophical premises, and neither they nor their beliefs are disparaged here. But when that sincere, personal opposition becomes enacted law and public policy, the necessary consequence is to put the imprimatur of the State itself on an exclusion that soon demeans or stigmatizes those whose own liberty is then denied. Under the Constitution, same-sex couples seek in marriage the same legal treatment as opposite-sex couples, and it would disparage their choices and diminish their personhood to deny them this right.

The right of same-sex couples to marry that is part of the liberty promised by the Fourteenth Amendment is derived, too, from that Amendment's guarantee of the equal protection of the laws. The Due Process Clause and the Equal Protection Clause are connected in a profound way, though they set forth independent principles. Rights implicit in liberty and rights secured by equal protection may rest on different precepts and are not always co-extensive, yet in some instances each may be instructive as to the meaning and reach of the other. [T]he right to marry is a fundamental right inherent in the liberty of the person, and under the Due Process and Equal Protection Clauses of the Fourteenth Amendment couples of the same-sex may not be deprived of that right and that liberty. The Court now holds that same-sex couples may exercise the fundamental right to marry. No longer may this liberty be denied to them. *Baker* v. *Nelson* must be and now is overruled, and the State laws challenged by Petitioners in these cases are now held invalid to the extent they exclude same-sex couples from civil marriage on the same terms and conditions as opposite-sex couples.

There may be an initial inclination in these cases to proceed with caution—to await further legislation, litigation, and debate. . . . Yet there has been far more deliberation than this argument acknowledges. There have been referenda, legislative debates, and grassroots campaigns, as well as countless studies, papers, books, . . . extensive litigation in state and federal courts . . . more than 100 *amici* [briefs].

[T]he Constitution contemplates that democracy is the appropriate process for change, so long as that process does not abridge fundamental rights. . . . The dynamic of our constitutional system is that individuals need not await legislative action before asserting a fundamental right. The Nation's courts are open to injured individuals who come to them to vindicate their own direct, personal stake in our basic charter. An individual can invoke a right to constitutional protection when he or she is harmed, even if the broader public disagrees and even if the legislature refuses to act. . . .

Finally, it must be emphasized that religions, and those who adhere to religious doctrines, may continue to advocate with utmost, sincere conviction that, by divine precepts, same-sex marriage should not be condoned. The First Amendment ensures that religious organizations and persons are given proper protection as they seek to teach the principles that are so fulfilling and so central to their lives and faiths, and to their own deep aspirations to continue the family structure they have long revered. The same is true of those who oppose same-sex marriage for other reasons. In turn, those who believe allowing same-sex marriage is proper or indeed essential, whether as a matter of religious conviction or secular belief, may engage those who disagree with their view in an open and searching debate. The Constitution, however, does not permit the State to bar same-sex couples from marriage on the same terms as accorded to couples of the opposite sex.

. . . Leaving the current state of affairs in place would maintain and promote instability and uncertainty. For some couples, even an ordinary drive into a neighboring State to visit family or friends risks causing severe hardship in the event of a spouse's hospitalization while across state lines. In light of the fact that many States already allow same-sex marriage—and hundreds of thousands of these marriages already have occurred—the disruption caused by the recognition bans is significant and ever-growing. . . . The Court, in this decision, holds same-sex couples may exercise the fundamental right to marry in all States. It follows that . . . there is no lawful basis for a State to refuse to recognize a lawful same-sex marriage performed in another State on the ground of its same-sex character. . . . The judgment of the Court of Appeals for the Sixth Circuit is reversed. It is so ordered.

CHIEF JUSTICE ROBERTS, with whom JUSTICE SCALIA and JUSTICE THOMAS join, dissenting.

[T]his Court is not a legislature. Whether same-sex marriage is a good idea should be of no concern to us. Under the Constitution, judges have power to say what the law is, not what it should be. The people who ratified the Constitution authorized courts to exercise "neither force nor will but merely judgment." The Federalist No. 78.

Although the policy arguments for extending marriage to same-sex couples may be compelling, the legal arguments for requiring such an extension are not. The fundamental right to marry does not include a right to make a State change its definition of marriage. And a State's decision to maintain the meaning of marriage that has persisted in every culture throughout human history can hardly be called irrational. In short, our Constitution does not enact any one theory of marriage. The people of a State are free to expand marriage to include same-sex couples, or to retain the historic definition.

Today, however, the Court takes the extraordinary step of ordering every State to license and recognize same-sex marriage. Many people will rejoice at this decision, and I begrudge none their celebration. But for those who believe in a government of laws, not of men, the majority's approach is deeply disheartening. Supporters of same-sex marriage have achieved considerable success persuading their fellow citizens—through the democratic process—to adopt their view. That ends today. Five lawyers have closed the debate and enacted their own vision of marriage as a matter of constitutional law. Stealing this issue from the people will for many cast a cloud over same-sex marriage, making a dramatic social change that much more difficult to accept. [T]he Court invalidates the marriage laws of more than half the States and orders the transformation of a social institution that has formed the basis of human society for millennia, for the Kalahari Bushmen and the Han Chinese, the Carthaginians and the Aztecs. Just who do we think we are? . . .

Petitioners and their *amici* base their arguments on the "right to marry" and the imperative of "marriage equality." There is no serious dispute that, under our precedents, the Constitution protects a right to marry and requires States to apply their marriage laws equally. The real question in these cases is what constitutes "marriage," or—more precisely—*who decides* what constitutes "marriage"? [T]he majority acknowledges, marriage "has existed for millennia and across civilizations." For all those millennia, across all those civilizations, "marriage" referred to only one relationship: the union of a man and a woman. Tr. of Oral Arg. (petitioners conceding that they are not aware of any society that permitted same-sex marriage before 2001). . . . Marriage did not come about as a result of a political movement, discovery, disease, war, religious doctrine, or any other moving force of world history—and certainly not as a result of a prehistoric decision to exclude gays and lesbians. It arose in the nature of things to meet a vital need: ensuring that children are conceived by a mother and father committed to raising them in the stable conditions of a lifelong relationship. [F]or the good of children and society, sexual relations that can lead to procreation should occur only between a man and a woman committed to a lasting bond. Society has recognized that bond as marriage. And by bestowing a respected status and material benefits on married couples, society encourages men and women to conduct sexual relations within marriage rather than without. As one prominent scholar put it, "Marriage is a socially arranged solution for the problem of getting people to stay together and care for children that the mere desire for children, and the sex that makes children possible, does not solve." J. Q. Wilson, The Marriage Problem 41 (2002).

This singular understanding of marriage has prevailed in the United States throughout our history. . . . The Constitution itself says nothing about marriage, and the Framers thereby entrusted the States with "[t]he whole subject of the domestic relations of husband and wife." *Windsor*. There is no dispute that every State at the founding—and every State throughout our history until a dozen years ago—defined marriage in the traditional, biologically rooted way. . . .

Petitioners first contend that the marriage laws of their States violate the Due Process Clause. The Solicitor General of the United States, appearing in support of petitioners, expressly disowned that position before this Court. The majority nevertheless resolves these cases for petitioners based almost entirely on the Due Process Clause.

[T]he majority's approach has no basis in principle or tradition, except for the unprincipled tradition of judicial policymaking that characterized discredited decisions such as *Lochner* v. *New York*, 198 U.S. 45. Stripped of its shiny rhetorical gloss, the majority's argument is that the Due Process Clause gives same-sex couples a fundamental right to marry because it will be good for them and for society. If I were a legislator, I would certainly consider that view as a matter of social policy. But as a judge, I find the majority's position indefensible as a matter of constitutional law. . . .

Allowing unelected federal judges to select which unenumerated rights rank as "fundamental"—and to strike down state laws on the basis of that determination—raises obvious concerns about the judicial role. . . . One immediate question invited by the majority's position is whether States may retain the definition of marriage as a union of two people. Cf. *Brown* v. *Buhman*, 947 F. Supp. 2d 1170 (Utah 2013), appeal pending, No. 14–4117 (CA10). Although the majority randomly inserts the adjective "two" in various places, it offers no reason at all why the two-person element of the core definition of marriage may be preserved while the man-woman element may not. Indeed, from the standpoint of history and tradition, a leap from opposite-sex marriage to same-sex marriage is much greater than one from a two-person union to plural unions, which have deep roots in some cultures around the world. If the majority is willing to take the big leap, it is hard to see how it can say no to the shorter one.

It is striking how much of the majority's reasoning would apply with equal force to the claim of a fundamental right to plural marriage. If "[t]here is dignity in the bond between two men or two women who seek to marry and in their autonomy to make such profound choices," why would there be any less dignity in the bond between three people who, in exercising their autonomy, seek to make the profound choice to marry? If a same-sex couple has the constitutional right to marry because their children would otherwise "suffer the stigma of knowing their families are somehow lesser," why wouldn't the same reasoning apply to a family of three or more persons raising children? If not having the opportunity to marry "serves to disrespect and subordinate" gay and lesbian couples, why wouldn't the same "imposition of this disability," serve to disrespect and subordinate people who find fulfillment in polyamorous relationships? See Bennett, Polyamory: The Next Sexual Revolution? Newsweek, July 28, 2009 (estimating 500,000 polyamorous families in the United States); Li, Married Lesbian "Throuple" Expecting First Child, N. Y. Post, Apr. 23, 2014; Otter, Three May Not Be a Crowd: The Case for a Constitutional Right to Plural Marriage, 64 Emory L. J. 1977 (2015).

Nowhere is the majority's extravagant conception of judicial supremacy more evident than in its description—and dismissal—of the public debate regarding same-sex marriage. Yes, the majority concedes, on one side are thousands of years of human history in every society known to have populated the planet. But on the other side, there has been "extensive litigation," "many thoughtful District Court decisions," "countless studies, papers, books, and other popular and scholarly writings," and "more than 100" *amicus* briefs in these cases alone. What would be the point of allowing the democratic process to go on? It is high time for the Court to decide the meaning of marriage, based on five lawyers' "better informed understanding" of "a liberty that remains urgent in our own era." The answer is surely there in one of those *amicus* briefs or studies.

Those who founded our country would not recognize the majority's conception of the judicial role. They after all risked their lives and fortunes for the precious right to govern themselves. [P]eople are in the midst of a serious and thoughtful public debate on the issue of same-sex marriage. They see voters carefully considering same-sex marriage, casting ballots in favor or opposed, and sometimes changing their minds. They see political leaders similarly reexamining their positions, and either reversing course or explaining adherence to old convictions confirmed anew. They see governments and businesses modifying policies and practices with respect to same-sex couples, and participating actively in the civic discourse. They see countries overseas democratically accepting profound social change, or declining to do so. This deliberative process is making people take seriously questions that they may not have even regarded as questions before. . . .

Respect for sincere religious conviction has led voters and legislators in every State that has adopted same-sex marriage democratically to include accommodations for religious practice. The majority's decision imposing same-sex marriage cannot, of course, create any such accommodations. The majority graciously suggests that religious believers may continue to "advocate" and "teach" their views of marriage. The First Amendment guarantees, however, the freedom to *"exercise"* religion. Ominously, that is not a word the majority uses. . . .

JUSTICE SCALIA, with whom JUSTICE THOMAS joins, dissenting.

. . . . Today's decree says that my Ruler, and the Ruler of 320 million Americans coast-to-coast, is a majority of the nine lawyers on the Supreme Court. The opinion in these cases is the furthest extension in fact—and the furthest extension one can even imagine—of the Court's claimed power to create "liberties" that the Constitution and its Amendments neglect to mention. This practice of constitutional revision by an unelected committee of nine, always accompanied (as it is today) by extravagant praise of liberty, robs the People of the most important liberty they asserted in the Declaration of Independence and won in the Revolution of 1776: the freedom to govern themselves. [E]lectorates of 11 States, either directly or through their representatives, chose to expand the traditional definition of marriage. Many more decided not to. Win or lose, advocates for both sides continued pressing their cases, secure in the knowledge that an electoral loss can be negated by a later electoral win. That is exactly how our system of government is supposed to work.

[T]he Court ends this debate, in an opinion lacking even a thin veneer of law. Buried beneath the mummeries and straining-to-be-memorable passages of the opinion is a candid and startling assertion: No matter *what* it was the People ratified, the Fourteenth Amendment protects those rights that the Judiciary, in its "reasoned judgment," thinks the Fourteenth Amendment ought to protect. That is so because "[t]he generations that wrote and ratified the Bill of Rights and the Fourteenth Amendment did not presume to know the extent of freedom in all of its dimensions . . ." One would think that sentence would continue: ". . . and therefore they provided for a means by which the People could amend the Constitution," or perhaps ". . . and therefore they left the creation of additional liberties, such as the freedom to marry someone of the same sex, to the People, through the never-ending process of legislation." But no. What logically follows, in the majority's judge-empowering estimation, is: "and so they entrusted to future generations a charter protecting the right of all persons to enjoy liberty as we learn its meaning." The "we," needless to say, is the nine of us. . . .

Judges are selected precisely for their skill as lawyers; whether they reflect the policy views of a particular constituency is not (or should not be) relevant. Not surprisingly then, the Federal Judiciary is hardly a cross-section of America. Take, for example, this Court, which consists of only nine men and women, all of them successful lawyers who studied at Harvard or Yale Law School. Four of the nine are natives of New York City. Eight of them grew up in east- and west-coast States. Only one hails from the vast expanse in-between. Not a single Southwesterner or even, to tell the truth, a genuine Westerner (California does not count). Not a single evangelical Christian (a group that comprises about one quarter of

Americans), or even a Protestant of any denomination. The strikingly unrepresentative character of the body voting on today's social upheaval would be irrelevant if they were functioning as *judges*, answering the legal question whether the American people had ever ratified a constitutional provision that was understood to proscribe the traditional definition of marriage. [T]o allow the policy question of same-sex marriage to be considered and resolved by a select, patrician, highly unrepresentative panel of nine is to violate a principle even more fundamental than no taxation without representation: no social transformation without representation.

But what really astounds is the hubris reflected in today's judicial Putsch. The five Justices who compose today's majority are entirely comfortable concluding that every State violated the Constitution for all of the 135 years between the Fourteenth Amendment's ratification and Massachusetts' permitting of same-sex marriages in 2003.

[The Court's] opinion is couched in a style that is as pretentious as its content is egotistic. It is one thing for separate concurring or dissenting opinions to contain extravagances, even silly extravagances, of thought and expression; it is something else for the official opinion of the Court to do so.[22] Of course the opinion's showy profundities are often profoundly incoherent. "The nature of marriage is that, through its enduring bond, two persons together can find other freedoms, such as expression, intimacy, and spirituality." (Really? Who ever thought that intimacy and spirituality [whatever that means] were freedoms? And if intimacy is, one would think Freedom of Intimacy is abridged rather than expanded by marriage. Ask the nearest hippie. Expression, sure enough, *is* a freedom, but anyone in a long-lasting marriage will attest that that happy state constricts, rather than expands, what one can prudently say.) . . .

JUSTICE THOMAS, with whom JUSTICE SCALIA joins, dissenting. . . .

Numerous *amici*—even some not supporting the States—have cautioned the Court that its decision here will "have unavoidable and wide-ranging implications for religious liberty." In our society, marriage is not simply a governmental institution; it is a religious institution as well. Today's decision might change the former, but it cannot change the latter. [T]he two will come into conflict, particularly as individuals and churches are confronted with demands to participate in and endorse civil marriages between same-sex couples. . . . Religious liberty is about freedom of action in matters of religion generally, and the scope of that

---

[22] If, even as the price to be paid for a fifth vote, I ever joined an opinion for the Court that began: "The Constitution promises liberty to all within its reach, a liberty that includes certain specific rights that allow persons, within a lawful realm, to define and express their identity," I would hide my head in a bag. The Supreme Court of the United States has descended from the disciplined legal reasoning of John Marshall and Joseph Story to the mystical aphorisms of the fortune cookie.

liberty is directly correlated to the civil restraints placed upon religious practice. . . .

JUSTICE ALITO, with whom JUSTICE SCALIA and JUSTICE THOMAS join, dissenting. . . .

Today's decision usurps the constitutional right of the people to decide whether to keep or alter the traditional understanding of marriage. [It also] will be used to vilify Americans who are unwilling to assent to the new orthodoxy. [T]he majority attempts, toward the end of its opinion, to reassure those who oppose same-sex marriage that their rights of conscience will be protected. We will soon see whether this proves to be true. I assume that those who cling to old beliefs will be able to whisper their thoughts in the recesses of their homes, but if they repeat those views in public, they will risk being labeled as bigots and treated as such by governments, employers, and schools. . . . Recalling the harsh treatment of gays and lesbians in the past, some may think that turnabout is fair play. But if that sentiment prevails, the Nation will experience bitter and lasting wounds. . . . Most Americans—understandably—will cheer or lament today's decision [b]ut all Americans, whatever their thinking on that issue, should worry about what the majority's claim of power portends.

NOTES

1. The majority never says that sexual orientation is a suspect class, subject to strict scrutiny. Is sexual orientation now a suspect class?

Runyon v. McCrary, 427 U.S. 160 (1976) [Casebook, § 9–2], held a federal law, 42 U.S.C.A § 1981, forbids racial discrimination in making private contracts. It also specifically said that it was not interpreting that statute to apply to private schools "that practice racial exclusion on religious grounds." *Heart of Atlanta Motel, Inc. v. United States*, 379 U.S. 241 (1964) [Casebook § 4–4], upheld federal commerce power to prohibit racial discrimination in places of public accommodation, and noted that law exempted landlords who lived in the building and offered "not more than five rooms for rent." This statutory exemption exists to this day. In *Hurley v. Irish-American Gay, Lesbian and Bisexual Group of Boston*, 515 U.S. 557 (1995) [Casebook unabridged, § 10–9.4, abridged], § 10–9.2, gay, lesbian, and bisexual descendants of Irish immigrants sought to march as a group in the St. Patrick's Day parade. The parade's private organizers refused and the state supreme court held that this exclusion violated Massachusetts' public accommodation law, which prohibits discrimination on account of, inter alia, sexual orientation, in places of public accommodation. Souter, J, for a unanimous Court, held that when Massachusetts required the defendants to alter the expressive content of their parade, it violated the First Amendment.

Should such cases apply to individuals who (on free speech or free exercise grounds) do not want to participate in gay marriages? For example, the state could provide that the baker cannot refuse to sell a cupcake to a customer because the customer is gay. [The parade organizers in *Hurley* did not exclude gays as individuals; they did exclude a gay pride float.] However, the baker may argue that creating a wedding cake (unlike selling a cupcake) is a work of art and participating in the wedding, thus a part of free speech. Is participating (or refusing to participate) in a wedding part of free expression, like a parade that excludes a gay pride float?

Consider wedding photographers. Taking a passport photo is not participating in the travel and it is not a work of art. Is taking a portfolio of wedding photos part of free expression? Could the photographer say, "I will not participate in your wedding by taking photographs because I do not believe in gay weddings"? Is that different from saying, "I will not participate in your wedding by taking photographs because you cuckolded me and now you are marrying my ex-wife"? Could the state force the cuckolded photographer to take the wedding photos? Or, "I will not participate in your wedding by taking photographs because you ran over my neighbor's dog 10 years ago"? May the state force the local baker to cater to a KKK rally? Could it force the gay baker to design and make a cake that says, "same sex marriage is morally wrong"?

Does it matter, in deciding these issues, whether or not *Obergefell* held that sexual orientation is a suspect class?

2. Justice Ginsburg, while on the D.C. Circuit, wrote a law review article arguing that *Roe v. Wade*, 410 U.S. 113 (1973), Casebook, unabridged, § 8–3.43; abridged, § 8–3.33, would have been more acceptable if the Court had not gone beyond a narrow ruling invalidating the particular statute in the case. "The political process was moving . . . , not swiftly enough for advocates of quick, complete change, but majoritarian institutions were listening and acting. Heavy-handed judicial intervention was difficult to justify and appears to have provoked, not resolved, conflict." Ginsburg, *Some Thoughts on Autonomy and Equality in Relation to Roe v. Wade*, 63 N. C. L. Rev. 375, 385–86 (1985) (footnote omitted). Should that argument apply to this case?

3. Chief Justice Roberts' dissent cites *Brown v. Buhman*, 947 F. Supp. 2d 1170 (Utah 2013), vacated as moot, 822 F.3d 1151 (10th Cir. May 13, 2016)(county attorney's announcement of policy limiting bigamy prosecutions rendered case moot). In that case, a polygamist family challenged the constitutionality of Utah's bigamy statute. The district court held that the cohabitation prong of the statute was "unconstitutional on numerous grounds and strikes it." The court allowed the statute "to remain in force as prohibiting bigamy in the literal sense—the fraudulent or otherwise impermissible possession of two purportedly valid marriage licenses for the purpose of entering into more than one purportedly legal marriage." The TV reality series, *Sister Wives*, featured the plaintiffs, Kody Brown, his four wives, and 17 children. The 10th Circuit dismissed the appeal as moot.

4. *Pavan v. Smith*, 582 U.S. ___, 137 S.Ct. 2075, 198 L.Ed.2d 636 (2017)(per curiam), summarily reversed the Arkansas Supreme Court and held that an Arkansas' birth certificate scheme violates *Obergefell*. Two married same-sex couples conceived children through anonymous sperm donation. An Arkansas statute generally required the name of mother's male spouse to appear on child's birth certificate when mother conceived a child by means of artificial insemination but it allowed omission of mother's female spouse from her child's birth certificate. Plaintiffs sued, arguing that this legislative scheme violated the Constitution

The divided Arkansas Supreme Court upheld the scheme arguing, "the statute centers on the relationship of the biological mother and the biological father to the child, not on the marital relationship of husband and wife," and "does not run afoul of *Obergefell*." The Court rejected that argument. "[S]tate law, as interpreted by the court below, allows Arkansas officials in those very same circumstances to omit a married woman's female spouse from her child's birth certificate." "*Obergefell* proscribes such disparate treatment."

Gorsuch, J., joined by Thomas & Alito, JJ., dissented, arguing that summary reversal was an inappropriate way to decide that a state "birth registration scheme based on biology" violates *Obergefell*. Particularly where, as here, "the State has repeatedly conceded that the benefits afforded nonbiological parents under § 9–10–201 must be afforded equally to both same-sex and opposite-sex couples."

CHAPTER 10

FREEDOM OF SPEECH

■ ■ ■

10–3 TIME, PLACE, AND MANNER RESTRICTIONS AND THE PUBLIC FORUM

10–3.2 PROTECTION OF THE PUBLIC FROM FRAUD AND ANNOYANCE

Unabridged, p. 1068; add to end of *Notes,* new Note 4:

4. PROFESSIONAL SPEECH. *National Institute of Life Advocates v. Becerra,* 138 S.Ct. 2361, 201 L.Ed.2d 835 (2018). A California law regulates crisis pregnancy centers—pro-life centers that offer pregnancy-related services. The law requires clinics that primarily serve pregnant women to provide certain notices. Clinics that are licensed must notify women that California provides free or low-cost services, including abortions. Unlicensed clinics must notify women that California has not licensed the clinics to provide medical services. A licensed and an unlicensed clinic challenged the law as violating their First Amendment right to free speech. Lower courts denied their request for a preliminary injunction, concluding that the licensed notice survived a lower level of scrutiny applicable to regulations of "professional speech," and the unlicensed notice satisfied any level of scrutiny. The Supreme Court (5–4) reversed. Thomas, J., joined by Roberts, C.J., Kennedy, Alito, and Gorsuch, JJ., held that the notice requirement was a content-based regulation that compelled petitioners to deliver a particular message, namely, to advertise abortion, the very practice that petitioners strongly oppose. The law could be justified only if it was narrowly tailored to serve compelling state interests, and the law did not meet that test. With respect to the unlicensed notice, the lower courts applied a less demanding standard, again because they concluded the law regulated "professional speech." However, as the majority observed, professional speech is a difficult category to define with precision, and the Court has never recognized a separate category of speech merely because it is uttered by professionals. The Court identified two circumstances in which it has afforded less protection for professional speech: first, where a law requires professionals to disclose factual, noncontroversial information in their commercial speech [*Zauderer v. Office of Disciplinary Counsel of Supreme Court of Ohio*, 471 U.S. 626, 651 (1985)] and second, where a state regulates professional conduct that incidentally involves speech [*Ohralik v. Ohio State Bar Assn.*, 436 U.S. 447, 456 (1978)].

Neither situation is implicated under the licensed notice because the notice is not limited to "purely factual and noncontroversial information," nor is it a regulation of professional conduct that incidentally burdens speech. The licensed notice deals with providing pregnant women with information about state-sponsored abortion services, hardly an "uncontroversial" topic, and it is not a regulation of professional conduct in which a physician is required to "give a woman certain information as part of obtaining her consent to an abortion." *Planned Parenthood of Southeastern Pa. v. Casey*, 505 U.S. 833, 884 (1992). The regulation also is "wildly underinclusive" because it applies to only a very narrow subset of clinics whose "primary purpose" is to provide family planning and pregnancy-related services. Many other clinics that have another primary purpose also serve low income women but are exempt from the notice requirement without any explanation. Strict scrutiny is appropriate to review content-based regulations of professional speech which pose a risk, as in this case, "that the Government seeks not to advance a legitimate regulatory goal, but to suppress unpopular ideas or information." The unlicensed notice also unduly burdens protected speech and California has not demonstrated any justification for the unlicensed notice that is more than "purely hypothetical"—ensuring that women know when they are receiving medical care from licensed professionals. Even so, the regulation imposes a government-scripted, speaker-based disclosure requirement wholly disconnected from the State's informational interest and covering a very narrow subset of speakers, those that primarily provide pregnancy-related services.

Kennedy, J., joined by Roberts, C.J., and Alito and Gorsuch, JJ., concurred "to underscore that the apparent viewpoint discrimination here is a matter of serious constitutional concern." By requiring primarily pro-life pregnancy centers to promote the State's preferred message advertising abortions, the State "compels individuals to contradict their most deeply held beliefs." "The history of the Act's enactment and its underinclusive application suggest a real possibility that these individuals were targeted because of their beliefs."

Breyer, J., joined by Ginsburg, Sotomayor, and Kagan, JJ., dissented. The majority's use of strict scrutiny to review the disclosure law is unwarranted and invites courts "to apply an unpredictable First Amendment to ordinary social and economic regulations." Indeed, since the Court's departure from the discredited approach under *Lochner v. New York*, 198 U.S. 45 (1905), "ordinary economic and social legislation has been thought to raise little constitutional concern." Under the Court's view in the instant case, "[v]irtually every disclosure law could be considered 'content based' for virtually every disclosure law requires individuals 'to speak a particular message'." *Reed v. Town of Gilbert*, 135 S.Ct. 2218, 2234–2235 (2015)(Breyer, J., concurring)(listing regulations that involve content discrimination, ranging from securities regulations to signs in petting zoos). Recognizing the problem that if taken literally the majority's view could radically change disclosure law, the majority adds a general disclaimer that "does not question the legality of health and safety warnings" or "purely factual and noncontroversial disclosure about commercial products." However, the dissent observes, the majority does not explain why the California law does not fall into the majority's "health" category. If the Court in *Planned Parenthood of Southeastern Pa. v. Casey* saw no constitutional infirmity in the requirement that the physician provide information about the risks of abortion and childbirth in a manner mandated by the state, "the law's demand for evenhandedness requires a different answer" than that given by the Court. "If a state can lawfully require a doctor to tell a woman seeking an abortion about adoption services, why should it not be able, as here, to require a medical counselor to tell a woman seeking prenatal care or other reproductive healthcare about childbirth and abortion services?"

The majority's contention that the disclosure here is unrelated to a medical procedure as in *Casey,* and so the state has no reason to inform a woman about alternatives to childbirth, according to the dissent, is disingenuous. "No one doubts that choosing an abortion is a medical procedure that involves certain health risks." Indeed, the dissent points out, childbirth is 14 times more likely than abortion to result in a woman's death. Moreover, that the majority finds it "telling" that paid clinics are not required to provide the licensed notice is hardly surprising. The lack-of-information problem the California law sought to ameliorate is commonly found among low-income women who would find the information about financial assistance particularly useful. Indeed, "the value to consumers of the information such speech provides" is "the reason that the First Amendment protects commercial speech at all." There is "minimal" First Amendment interest in not providing factual information to patients. "[A] Constitution that allows States to insist that medical providers tell women about the possibility of adoption should also allow States similarly to insist that medical providers tell women about the possibility of abortion." Finally, as the dissent sees it, the majority's claim that many licensed healthcare clinics are exempted from the law so as to make the law underinclusive is not convincing. In terms of the law's informational objective, the exempted clinics appear to provide the entire spectrum of services required of the notice and therefore there would be no need to cover them. Nor is there evidence in the record to suggest that the unlicensed notice law burdens only pro-life conduct and therefore unconstitutionally discriminates on the basis of viewpoint. Indeed, the law on its face does not distinguish between pro-life and pro-choice viewpoints. The law does not single out pregnancy-related facilities for the disclosure requirement. The law seeks to ensure that pregnant women know when they are getting medical care from licensed professionals.

10–3.3 DEFINING THE PUBLIC FORUM

Unabridged, p. 1078; add at end of Note 5:

Minnesota Voters Alliance v. Mansky, 138 S.Ct. 1876 (2018). Numerous states prohibit wearing various kinds of campaign-related clothing and accessories in a polling place on Election Day. Minnesota, one of these states, prohibits individuals from wearing political badges, buttons, or other political insignia inside polling places. Election judges monitor the so-called "political apparel ban" and can subject violators to civil and criminal penalties. Lower courts upheld the ban but the Supreme Court, in an opinion by Chief Justice Roberts (7–2), held the ban unconstitutional as a violation of free speech. The polling place is a non-public forum and some content-based restrictions on speech, including restrictions that exclude political advocacy, will be upheld if they are reasonable in light of the purpose served by the forum, here, voting. The Court agreed that as in *Burson*, some forms of campaign advocacy should be excluded from both outside and inside the polling place in order to set it aside as "an island of calm in which voters can peacefully contemplate their choices." Indeed, the designation of an area for voters within the polling place as "their own" is a more significant interest than outside. And the Court agreed with Minnesota that some kinds of campaign-related clothing and accessories should stay outside. However, the line a state draws must be reasonable and provide a sensible basis for determining what may come in and what must stay out. The Minnesota statute is too indeterminate; it does not define "political" and the "unmoored use of the term" and "haphazard interpretations" are confusing and raise more questions than answers. Would any message relating to the structure or affairs of government be covered? Would any issue that a candidate has ever discussed be covered? Would any item promoting the political "views" of any group be covered? And will election judges have the requisite knowledge and experience about these questions to enforce the ban responsibly? There is too much potential for erratic application and the opportunity for abuse. In sum, "Minnesota has not supported its good intentions with a law capable of reasoned application."

Sotomayor, J., joined by Breyer, J. dissented, arguing that there is a substantial amount of speech that clearly qualifies as political and before striking down the statute, the Court should have given Minnesota's highest court an opportunity to construe the statute within constitutional bounds.

Unabridged, p. 1078; add to end of *Notes*, new Note 6:

6. SIGNS. *Reed v. Town of Gilbert*, 576 U.S. ___, 135 S.Ct. 2218, 192 L.Ed.2d 236 (2015). Thomas, J., for the Court, reversed the Ninth Circuit. There were no dissents. Town of Gilbert's sign ordinance is an unconstitutional, content-based regulation of speech. The town has a comprehensive sign code prohibiting the display of outdoor signs without a permit. It includes 23 exemptions, three of which apply to ideological, political, and temporary directional signs. While all three exemptions include various restrictions on size and/or time and placement, the temporary directional signs have greater restrictions than either the ideological or political signs. The Good News Community Church holds services at different facilities because it does not have a permanent church. It uses temporary directional signs to invite people to services. The law provides that these signs may not be bigger than 6 square feet and can go up only 12 hours before their Sunday services start, which means that the church cannot post the signs until late on Saturday night when they are harder to see in the dark. The restrictions "depend entirely on the communicative content of the sign." For example, the Town treats differently a sign informing its reader of the time and place that a book club will discuss John Locke's Two Treatises of Government from a sign expressing the view that one should vote for one of Locke's followers in an upcoming election. "More to the point, the Church's signs inviting people to attend its worship services are treated differently from signs conveying other types of ideas. On its face, the Sign Code is a content-based regulation of speech." Placing strict limits on temporary directional signs is hardly necessary to beautify the Town when other types of signs create the same problem. Nor has the Town shown that temporary directional signs pose a greater threat to public safety than ideological or political signs.

The Town has ample "content-neutral options" available to resolve problems with safety and aesthetics, such as size, building materials, lighting, moving parts, and portability. The Town can also forbid posting signs on public property, so long as it does so in an evenhanded, content-neutral manner.

10–3.4 GOVERNMENT SUBSIDIZATION OF SPEECH [UNABRIDGED]

10–3.3 GOVERNMENT SUBSIDIZATION OF SPEECH [ABRIDGED]

Unabridged, p. 1086; add to *Notes,* new Note 5:

Abridged, p. 848: add to *Notes,* new Note 4:

Walker v. Texas Division, Sons of Confederate Veterans, Inc., 576 U.S. ___, 135 S.Ct. 2239, 192 L.Ed.2d 274 (2015). Texas allows automobile owners to choose a general-issue license plate or a specialty license plate (at an additional fee). The Confederate Veterans sued because Texas rejected a proposed specialty license plate design featuring a Confederate battle flag. Breyer, J., for the Court (5 to 4) held Texas's specialty license plate designs constitute government speech, and thus Texas was entitled to refuse to issue plates. Texas did not violate the nonprofit organization's free speech rights by denying its application for a design that included the Confederate flag. Texas "need not issue plates praising Florida's oranges as far better." Texas offers plates that say, "Fight Terrorism," but "it need not issue plates promoting al Qaeda." Drivers who display a State's selected license plate designs convey the messages communicated through those designs. The state could not compel a private party to express a view with which the private party disagrees, *Wooley v. Maynard,* 430 U.S. 705, 97 S.Ct. 1428, 51 L.Ed.2d 752 (1977)(state cannot require motor vehicles to bear license plates embossed with the state motto, "Live Free or Die"). Similarly, the Sons of Confederate

Veterans cannot force Texas to include a Confederate battle flag on its specialty license plates. "Texas license plates are, essentially, government IDs. And issuers of ID 'typically do not permit' the placement on their IDs of 'message[s] with which they do not wish to be associated,'" quoting *Summum*.

Alito, J., dissented, joined by Roberts, C.J., Scalia & Kennedy, JJ. "Here is a test. Suppose you sat by the side of a Texas highway and studied the license plates on the vehicles passing by. You would see, in addition to the standard Texas plates, an impressive array of specialty plates. (There are now more than 350 varieties.) You would likely observe plates that honor numerous colleges and universities. You might see plates bearing the name of a high school, a fraternity, or sorority, the Masons, the Knights of Columbus, the Daughters of the American Revolution, a realty company, a favorite soft drink, a favorite burger restaurant, and a favorite NASCAR driver." He then asked, "would you really think that the sentiments reflected in these specialty plates are the views of the State of Texas and not those of the owners of the cars?" How would you respond to that argument?

TRADEMARKS. *Matal v. Tam*, 582 U.S. ___, 137 S.Ct. 1744, 198 L.Ed.2d 366 (2017). A trademark applicant objected when the Patent and Trademark Office refused to register its trademark "THE SLANTS" (an Asian rock band) because that mark disparaged people of Asian descent. Alito, J., for the Court, held that disparagement clause of the Lanham Act, prohibiting federal trademark registration for marks that might disparage any persons, living or dead, was facially invalid under the First Amendment.[1] The "PTO has denied registration to 'Abort the Republicans' (disparaging to Republicans), 'Democrats Shouldn't Breed' (disparaging to Democrats), and a logo consisting of the communist hammer-and-sickle with a slash through it (disparaging to Soviets)."[2]

Matal held that trademarks are not government speech: "The Federal Government does not dream up these marks, and it does not edit marks submitted for registration." Moreover, the "government speech" doctrine is "susceptible to dangerous misuse." "If private speech could be passed off as government speech by simply affixing a government seal of approval, government could silence or muffle the expression of disfavored viewpoints."

A separate opinion of Alito, J., joined by Roberts, C.J., and Thomas, & Breyer, JJ., also rejected the government's argument that trademarks are subsidized speech because this case does not involve cash subsidies. They added it was unnecessary to decide if trademarks are Commercial Speech

---

[1]   In addition, Alito, J., joined by Roberts, C.J., Thomas & Breyer, JJ., wrote a concurring opinion. Kennedy, J. concurred in part and concurred in the judgment, joined by Ginsburg, Sotomayor, & Kagan, JJ. Thomas, J., filed an opinion concurring in part and concurring in the judgment. Justice Gorsuch took no part in the consideration or decision of the case.

[2]   Amicus Brief of Brief of the Cato Institute and a Basket of Deplorable People and Organizations as Amici Curiae Supporting Respondent, in *Lee v. Tam*, 2016 WL 7405919 (December 16, 2016, U.S.)

because the disparagement clause cannot survive the lessened scrutiny the Court applies in Commercial Speech cases. They added:

> An amicus supporting the Government refers to "encouraging racial tolerance and protecting the privacy and welfare of individuals." Brief for Native American Organizations as Amici Curiae 21. But no matter how the point is phrased, its unmistakable thrust is this: The Government has an interest in preventing speech expressing ideas that offend. And, as we have explained, that idea strikes at the heart of the First Amendment. Speech that demeans on the basis of race, ethnicity, gender, religion, age, disability, or any other similar ground is hateful; but the proudest boast of our free speech jurisprudence is that we protect the freedom to express "the thought that we hate."

Kennedy's separate opinion agreed that the disparagement clause constitutes viewpoint discrimination because it reflects the government's disapproval of certain speech, and that heightened scrutiny should apply, whether or not trademarks are commercial speech.

Iancu v. Brunetti, 139 S.Ct. 2294, 202 L.Ed.2d 510 (2019). Another provision in the Lanham Act [see *Matal* v. *Tam,* 137 S.Ct. 1744 (2017)(striking down provision in Lanham Act banning trademarks that disparage people] prohibits the registration of "immoral" or "scandalous" trademarks. Erik Brunetti, an artist and entrepreneur, founded a clothing line with the brand name F-U-C-T which, the Court noted, is "the equivalent of the past participle of a well-known word of profanity." Although registration of a mark is not mandatory and the owner of an unregistered mark may still use it in commerce, registration does give the owner valuable benefits in patent and infringement litigation. The Patent and Trade Office (PTO) refused to register Brunetti's trade mark under its test which asks whether a "substantial composite of the general public" would find the mark "shocking to the sense of truth, decency, or propriety"; "giving offense to the conscience or moral feelings"; "calling for condemnation"; "disgraceful"; "offensive"; "disreputable"; or "vulgar." Brunetti's facial challenge to the PTO's bar in the Court of Appeals for the Federal Circuit was successful and the Supreme Court affirmed. Kagan, J., joined by Thomas, Ginsburg, Alito, Gorsuch and Kavanaugh, JJ., held that the ban violates the First Amendment as a viewpoint-based restriction on speech. As in *Matal v. Tam,* the Court restated a bedrock postulate of free speech law: "The government may not discriminate against speech based on the ideas or opinions it conveys." The "immoral or scandalous" criterion in the Lanham Act is viewpoint-based. Together, the terms distinguish between two sets of ideas: "those aligned with conventional moral standards and those hostile to them; those inducing societal nods of approval and those provoking offense and condemnation." The government argued for a limiting construction that would remove the viewpoint bias so that marks could be banned "that are offensive or shocking to a substantial segment of the public because of their *mode* of expression, independent of any views that they mat express." The

Court rejected the proposal because "the statute says something markedly different;" the immoral and scandalous bar "stretches far beyond the government's proposed construction." Indeed, "to cut the statute off where the Government urges is not to interpret the statute Congress enacted, but to fashion a new one."

In a concurring opinion, Justice Alito noted that Congress could adopt a more carefully focused statute that precludes registration of marks "containing vulgar terms that play no real part in the expression of ideas" and that "the particular mark in question in this case could be denied registration under such a statute." That particular term "is not needed to express any idea and, in fact, as commonly used today, generally signifies nothing except emotion and a severely limited vocabulary." Chief Justice Roberts concurred and dissented. He believed the terms "immoral" and "scandalous" should be analyzed separately, and that while "immoral" is not susceptible of a narrowing construction, "scandalous" can be read to bar marks that offend not because of the ideas they convey but because of their mode of expression—marks that are obscene, vulgar or profane. Justice Breyer also concurred and dissented. He argued that the Court should treat First Amendment questions not strictly based on categories but more directly from values the First Amendment seeks to protect. He would ask whether the regulation works harm to First Amendment interests that is disproportionate in light of the relevant regulatory objectives. Thus, banning registration of "scandalous" marks works little harm. Such attention-grabbing highly vulgar words have an emotional and psychological impact that may distract consumers and disrupt business, and the government has a clear interest in seeking to disincentivize the use of such words. By contrast, banning "immoral" marks violates the First Amendment. Justice Sotomayor, joined by Justice Breyer, concurred and dissented. Noting that the line between viewpoint-based and viewpoint-neutral content-based discrimination is "slippery," a restriction on trademarks featuring obscenity, vulgarity, or profanity is viewpoint neutral although content-based. She agrees with Justice Breyer that the terms "immoral" is unconstitutional viewpoint based discrimination but that "scandalous" qualifies as a reasonable viewpoint-neutral, content-based regulation and can be separated and given a limiting construction.

10–4 FIGHTING WORDS AND HOSTILE AUDIENCES

Unabridged, p. 1107; at the end of case, add new *Note*:

Abridged, p. 863; add to end of *Notes*, new Note 3:

Elonis v. United States, 576 U.S. ___, 135 S.Ct. 2001, 192 L.Ed.2d 1 (2015). Elonis posted rap lyrics on his Facebook page containing graphically violent language and imagery about his ex-wife, coworkers, a kindergarten class, and state and federal law enforcement. His posts included disclaimers stating that the lyrics were fictitious and that he was exercising his First Amendment rights. Many people who knew him viewed his posts as threatening. His boss fired him for threatening co-workers, and his wife obtained a state court protection-from-abuse order against him. The FBI monitored him and eventually arrested him. The jury convicted him of violating 18 U.S.C. § 875(c), which makes it a crime to transmit in interstate commerce "any communication containing any threat" to "injure the person of another." The jury instruction was that Elonis was guilty if a *reasonable person* would interpret his statements as a threat. That instruction did not require the jury to determine the defendant's "mental state."

Chief Justice Roberts, for the Court, reversed and held that courts should generally interpret criminal statutes to include a *scienter* requirement and *mens rea* even when the statute does not contain them. Did the speaker act with a *subjective* intent to threaten? A " 'reasonable person' standard is a familiar feature of civil liability in tort law, but is inconsistent with 'the conventional requirement for criminal conduct—*awareness* of some wrongdoing.' " (Emphasis in original). Given the statutory interpretation, "it is not necessary to consider any First Amendment issues."

10–9   THE RIGHT OF ASSOCIATION

10–9.3 PATRONAGE DISMISSALS

Unabridged, p. 1196; add to end of *Notes*, new Note 7:

7.   *Heffernan v. City of Patterson*, 578 U.S. ___, 136 S.Ct. 1412, 194 L.Ed.2d 508 (2016). Jeffrey Heffernan, a police officer in Patterson, New Jersey, picked up, at the request of his bedridden mother, a campaign sign of the candidate running against the sitting Patterson mayor. The candidate was also a friend of Heffernan's. Other members of the Patterson police force saw him, sign in hand, talking to campaign workers, and so the chief of police and Heffernan's supervisor (both of whom the incumbent mayor had appointed) learned about it. The next day, Heffernan's supervisors demoted him from detective to patrol officer. He sued the City, claiming that the police chief and supervisor had deprived him of a "right . . . secured by the Constitution" in violation of 42 U.S.C. § 1983. The district court and Third Circuit ruled against Heffernan, concluding that although the defendants demoted him because they thought he was engaging in political activity (which is constitutionally protected), he was not, in fact, engaged in a constitutionally protected activity. The Court (6 to 2) reversed. Breyer, J., for the Court held that motive of the employer, not the employee, is key because the First Amendment prevents the employer from retaliating against Heffernan based on its mistaken belief that he had engaged in protected speech. This rule tracks the language of the First Amendment, which focuses on the Government's activity. Moreover, the constitutional harm (discouraging employees from engaging in protected speech) is the same, whether or not the employer's action rests on a factual mistake.

The employee still bears the burden of proving an improper employer motive. It is possible that the employer demoted Heffernan because of a neutral policy prohibiting him from overt involvement in any political campaign. The Court remanded for the lower courts to decide if that policy existed, whether Heffernan's supervisors followed it, and whether that standard is constitutional.

Thomas, J., joined by Alito J., dissented and argued that the City, although it demoted Heffernan to retaliate against his political beliefs, did not violate free speech because Heffernan did not intend to engage in First Amendment activity.

10–9.4 REGULATING THE MEMBERSHIP OF ASSOCIATIONS [UNABRIDGED]

10–9.2 REGULATING THE MEMBERSHIP OF ASSOCIATIONS [ABRIDGED]

Unabridged, p. 1229; after *Harris v. Quinn*, add new case:

Abridged, p. 942; after *Harris v. Quinn*, add new case:

JANUS V. AMERICAN FEDERATION OF STATE, COUNTY, AND MUNICIPAL EMPLOYEES, COUNCIL 31, ET AL.
138 S.Ct. 2448, 201 L.Ed.2d 924 (2018).

JUSTICE ALITO delivered the opinion of the Court.

Under Illinois law, public employees are forced to subsidize a union, even if they choose not to join and strongly object to the positions the union takes in collective bargaining and related activities. We conclude that this arrangement violates the free speech rights of nonmembers by compelling them to subsidize private speech on matters of substantial public concern.

We upheld a similar law in *Abood v. Detroit Bd. of Ed.*, 431 U.S. 209, 97 S.Ct. 1782, 52 L.Ed.2d 261 (1977), and we recognize the importance of following precedent unless there are strong reasons for not doing so. But there are very strong reasons in this case. Fundamental free speech rights are at stake. *Abood* was poorly reasoned. It has led to practical problems and abuse. It is inconsistent with other First Amendment cases and has been undermined by more recent decisions. Developments since *Abood* was handed down have shed new light on the issue of agency fees, and no reliance interests on the part of public-sector unions are sufficient to justify the perpetuation of the free speech violations that *Abood* has countenanced for the past 41 years. *Abood* is therefore overruled.

Under the Illinois Public Labor Relations Act, employees of the State and its political subdivisions are permitted to unionize. If a majority of the employees in a bargaining unit vote to be represented by a union, that union is designated as the exclusive representative of all the employees. Employees in the unit are not obligated to join the union selected by their co-workers, but whether they join or not, that union is deemed to be their sole permitted representative. Once a union is so designated, it is vested with broad authority. Only the union may negotiate with the employer on matters relating to "pay, wages, hours[,] and other conditions of employment. Designating a union as the employees' exclusive representative substantially restricts the rights of individual employees. Among other things, this designation means that individual employees may not be represented by any agent other than the designated union; nor may individual employees negotiate directly with their employer.

Employees who decline to join the union are not assessed full union dues but must instead pay what is generally called an "agency fee," which amounts to a percentage of the union dues. Under *Abood*, nonmembers may be charged for the portion of union dues attributable to activities that are "germane to [the union's] duties as collective-bargaining representative," but nonmembers may not be required to fund the union's political and ideological projects. In labor-law parlance, the outlays in the first category are known as "chargeable" expenditures, while those in the latter are labeled "nonchargeable."

Illinois law does not specify in detail which expenditures are chargeable and which are not. [The law] provides that an agency fee may compensate a union for the costs incurred in "the collective bargaining process, contract administration[,] and pursuing matters affecting wages, hours[,] and conditions of employment." Excluded from the agency-fee calculation are union expenditures "related to the election or support of any candidate for political office." Applying this standard, a union categorizes its expenditures as chargeable or nonchargeable and thus determines a nonmember's "proportionate share"; this determination is then audited; the amount of the "proportionate share" is certified to the employer; and the employer automatically deducts that amount from the nonmembers' wages. Nonmembers need not be asked, and they are not required to consent before the fees are deducted. As illustrated by the record in this case, unions charge nonmembers, not just for the cost of collective bargaining per se, but also for many other supposedly connected activities. Here, the nonmembers were told that they had to pay for "[l]obbying," "[s]ocial and recreational activities," "advertising," "[m]embership meetings and conventions," and "litigation," as well as other unspecified "[s]ervices" that "may ultimately inure to the benefit of the members of the local bargaining unit." The total chargeable amount for nonmembers was 78.06% of full union dues.

Petitioner Mark Janus is employed by the Illinois Department of Healthcare and Family Services as a child support specialist. The employees in his unit are among the 35,000 public employees in Illinois who are represented by respondent American Federation of State, County, and Municipal Employees, Council 31 (Union). Janus refused to join the Union because he opposes "many of the public policy positions that [it] advocates," including the positions it takes in collective bargaining. Janus believes that the Union's "behavior in bargaining does not appreciate the current fiscal crises in Illinois and does not reflect his best interests or the interests of Illinois citizens." Therefore, if he had the choice, he "would not pay any fees or otherwise subsidize [the Union]." Under his unit's collective-bargaining agreement, however, he was required to pay an agency fee of $44.58 per month, which would amount to about $535 per year.

[Janus filed a complaint alleging that all "nonmember fee deductions are coerced political speech" and that "the First Amendment forbids coercing any money from the nonmembers." The district court dismissed the complaint under the authority of *Abood* and the Seventh Circuit affirmed].

III

. . .The First Amendment, made applicable to the States by the Fourteenth Amendment, forbids abridgment of the freedom of speech. We have held time and again that freedom of speech "includes both the right to speak freely and the right to refrain from speaking at all." Compelling individuals to mouth support for views they find objectionable violates that cardinal constitutional command, and in most contexts, any such effort would be universally condemned. Perhaps because such compulsion so plainly violates the Constitution, most of our free speech cases have involved restrictions on what can be said, rather than laws compelling speech. But measures compelling speech are at least as threatening. Whenever the Federal Government or a State prevents individuals from saying what they think on important matters or compels them to voice ideas with which they disagree, it undermines these ends. When speech is compelled, however, additional damage is done. In that situation, individuals are coerced into betraying their convictions. Forcing free and independent individuals to endorse ideas they find objectionable is always demeaning, and for this reason, one of our landmark free speech cases said that a law commanding "involuntary affirmation" of objected-to beliefs would require "even more immediate and urgent grounds" than a law demanding silence. *West Virginia Bd. of Ed. v. Barnette*, 319 U.S. 624, 633 (1943). . . .

Compelling a person to subsidize the speech of other private speakers raises similar First Amendment concerns. . . . We have therefore recognized that a " 'significant impingement on First Amendment rights' " occurs when public employees are required to provide financial support for a union that "takes many positions during collective bargaining that have powerful political and civic consequences." *Knox v. Service Employees International Union [SEIU], Local 1000,* [Casebook, p. 1221].

Our free speech cases have identified "levels of scrutiny" to be applied in different contexts. In *Knox* and *Harris v. Quinn* [Casebook, p. 1223], [we]applied what we characterized as "exacting" scrutiny, Knox, a less demanding test than the "strict" scrutiny that might be thought to apply outside the commercial sphere. Under "exacting" scrutiny, we noted, a compelled subsidy must "serve a compelling state interest that cannot be achieved through means significantly less restrictive of associational freedoms.". . . [P]etitioner in the present case contends that the Illinois law at issue should be subjected to "strict scrutiny." The dissent, on the other hand, proposes that we apply what amounts to rational-basis review, that is, that we ask only whether a government employer could reasonably believe that the exaction of agency fees serves its interests. This form of minimal scrutiny is foreign to our free-speech jurisprudence, and we reject it here. At the same time, we again find it unnecessary to decide the issue of strict scrutiny because the Illinois scheme cannot survive under even the more permissive standard applied in *Knox* and *Harris*.

In *Abood*, the main defense of the agency-fee arrangement was that it served the State's interest in "labor peace." By "labor peace," the *Abood* Court meant avoidance of the conflict and disruption that it envisioned would occur if the employees in a unit were represented by more than one union. In such a situation, the Court predicted, "inter-union rivalries" would foster "dissension within the work force," and the employer could face "conflicting demands from different unions." Confusion would ensue if the employer entered into and attempted to "enforce two or more agreements specifying different terms and conditions of employment." And a settlement with one union would be "subject to attack from [a] rival labor organizatio[n]." We assume that "labor peace," in this sense of the term, is a compelling state interest, but *Abood* cited no evidence that the pandemonium it imagined would result if agency fees were not allowed, and it is now clear that *Abood*'s fears were unfounded. The *Abood* Court assumed that designation of a union as the exclusive representative of all the employees in a unit and the exaction of agency fees are inextricably linked, but that is simply not true.

The federal employment experience is illustrative. Under federal law, a union chosen by majority vote is designated as the exclusive representative of all the employees, but federal law does not permit agency fees. Nevertheless, nearly a million federal employees—about 27% of the federal work force—are union members. The situation in the Postal Service is similar. Although permitted to choose an exclusive representative, Postal Service employees are not required to pay an agency fee, and about 400,000 are union members. Likewise, millions of public employees in the 28 States that have laws generally prohibiting agency fees are represented by unions that serve as the exclusive representatives of all the employees. Whatever may have been the case 41 years ago when *Abood* was handed down, it is now undeniable that "labor peace" can readily be achieved "through means significantly less restrictive of associational freedoms" than the assessment of agency fees.

In addition to the promotion of "labor peace," *Abood* cited "the risk of 'free riders'" as justification for agency fees. Respondents and some of their *amici* endorse this reasoning, contending that agency fees are needed to prevent nonmembers from enjoying the benefits of union representation without shouldering the costs. Petitioner strenuously objects to this free-rider label. He argues that he is not a free rider on a bus headed for a destination that he wishes to reach but is more like a person shanghaied for an unwanted voyage. Whichever description fits the majority of public employees who would not subsidize a union if given the option, avoiding free riders is not a compelling interest. To hold otherwise across the board would have startling consequences. Many private groups speak out with the objective of obtaining government action that will have the effect of benefiting nonmembers. May all those who are thought to benefit from such efforts be compelled to subsidize this speech?. . . In simple terms, the First Amendment does not permit the government to compel a person to pay for another party's speech just because the government thinks that the speech furthers the interests of the person who does not want to pay.

Those supporting agency fees contend that the situation here is different because unions are statutorily required to "represen[t] the interests of all public employees in the unit," whether or not they are union members. We can think of two possible arguments. It might be argued that a State has a compelling interest in requiring the payment of agency fees because (1) unions would otherwise be unwilling to represent nonmembers or (2) it would be fundamentally unfair to require unions to provide fair representation for nonmembers if nonmembers were not required to pay. Neither of these arguments is sound. First, it is simply not true that unions will refuse to serve as the exclusive representative of all employees in the unit if they are not given agency fees. Even without agency fees, designation as the exclusive representative confers many benefits. As noted, that status gives the union a privileged place in negotiations over wages, benefits, and working conditions. . . . In addition, a union designated as exclusive representative is often granted special privileges, such as obtaining information about employees, and having dues and fees deducted directly from employee wages. The collective-bargaining agreement in this case guarantees a long list of additional privileges. These benefits greatly outweigh any extra burden imposed by the duty of providing fair representation for nonmembers. . . . What about the representation of nonmembers in grievance proceedings? Unions do not undertake this activity solely for the benefit of nonmembers—which is why Illinois law gives a public-sector union the right to send a representative to such proceedings even if the employee declines union representation. Representation of nonmembers furthers the union's interest in keeping control of the administration of the collective-bargaining agreement, since the resolution of one employee's grievance can affect others. . . . Nor can such fees be justified on the ground that it would otherwise be unfair to require a union to bear the duty of fair representation. That duty is a necessary concomitant of the authority that a union seeks when it chooses to serve as the exclusive representative of all the employees in a unit. . . .

IV

Implicitly acknowledging the weakness of *Abood*'s own reasoning, proponents of agency fees have come forward with alternative justifications for the decision, and we now address these arguments. The most surprising of these new arguments is the Union respondent's originalist defense of *Abood*. According to this argument, *Abood* was correctly decided because the First Amendment was not originally understood to provide any protection for the free speech rights of public employees. . . . The Union offers no persuasive founding-era evidence that public employees were understood to lack free speech protections. . . . The Union has also failed to show that, even if public employees enjoyed free speech rights, the First Amendment was nonetheless originally understood to allow forced subsidies like those at issue here. We can safely say that, at the time of the adoption of the First Amendment, no one gave any thought to whether public-sector unions could charge nonmembers agency fees. We do know, however, that prominent members of the founding generation condemned laws requiring public employees to affirm or support beliefs with which they disagreed.

The principal defense of *Abood* advanced by respondents and the dissent is based on our decision in *Pickering v. Board of Ed. of Township High School Dist. 205, Will Cty.*, 391 U.S. 563, 88 S.Ct. 1731, 20 L.Ed.2d 811 (1968), which held that a school district violated the First Amendment by firing a teacher for writing a letter critical of the school administration. Under *Pickering* and later cases in the same line, employee speech is largely unprotected if it is part of what the employee is paid to do, see *Garcetti v. Ceballos*, 547 U.S. 410, 421–422, 126 S.Ct. 1951, 164 L.Ed.2d 689 (2006), or if it involved a matter of only private concern, see *Connick v. Myers*, 461 U.S. 138, 146–149, 103 S.Ct. 1684 (1983). On the other hand, when a public employee speaks as a citizen on a matter of public concern, the employee's speech is protected unless " 'the interest of the state, as an employer, in promoting the efficiency of the public services it performs through its employees' outweighs 'the interests of the [employee], as a citizen, in commenting upon matters of public concern.'" *Harris,* 134 S.Ct., at 2642. *Pickering* was the centerpiece of the defense of *Abood* in *Harris*, and we found the argument unpersuasive. The intervening years have not improved its appeal. First, the *Pickering* framework was developed for use in a very different context—in cases that involve "one employee's speech and its impact on that employee's public responsibilities." This case, by contrast, involves a blanket requirement that all employees subsidize speech with which they may not agree. . . .

Second, the *Pickering* framework fits much less well where the government compels speech or speech subsidies in support of third parties. *Pickering* is based on the insight that the speech of a public-sector employee may interfere with the effective operation of a government office. When a public employer does not simply restrict potentially disruptive speech but commands that its employees mouth a message on its own behalf, the calculus is very different. Of course, if the speech in question is part of an employee's official duties, the employer may insist that the employee deliver any lawful message. Otherwise, however, it is not easy to imagine a situation in which a public employer has a legitimate need to demand that its employees recite words with which they disagree. . . .

Third, although both *Pickering* and *Abood* divided speech into two categories, the cases' categorization schemes do not line up. Superimposing the *Pickering* scheme on *Abood* would significantly change the *Abood* regime. Let us first look at speech that is not germane to collective bargaining but instead concerns political or ideological issues. Under *Abood,* a public employer is flatly prohibited from permitting nonmembers to be charged for this speech, but under Pickering, the employees' free speech interests could be overcome if a court found that the employer's interests outweighed the employees'. A similar problem arises with respect to speech that is germane to collective bargaining. The parties dispute how much of this speech is of public concern. Under *Abood*, nonmembers may be required to pay for all this speech, but *Pickering* would permit that practice only if the employer's interests outweighed those of the employees. Thus, recasting *Abood* as an application of *Pickering* would substantially alter the *Abood* scheme.

Even if we were to apply some form of *Pickering,* Illinois' agency-fee arrangement would not survive. . . . When an employee engages in speech that is part of the employee's job duties, the employee's words are really the words of the employer. The employee is effectively the employer's spokesperson. But when a union negotiates with the employer or represents employees in disciplinary proceedings, the union speaks for the employees, not the employer. Otherwise, the employer would be negotiating with itself and disputing its own actions. That is not what anybody understands to be happening. What is more, if the union's speech is really the employer's speech, then the employer could dictate what the union says. Unions, we trust, would be appalled by such a suggestion. The next step of the Pickering framework asks whether the speech is on a matter of public or only private concern. In *Harris*, the dissent's central argument in defense of *Abood* was that union speech in collective bargaining, including speech about wages and benefits, is basically a matter of only private interest. In addition to affecting how public money is spent, union speech in collective bargaining addresses many other important matters. Unions express views on a wide range of subjects—education, child welfare, healthcare, and minority rights, to name a few. What unions have to say on these matters in the context of collective bargaining is of great public importance. Unions can also speak out in collective bargaining on controversial subjects such as climate change, the Confederacy, sexual orientation and gender identity, evolution, and minority religions. These are sensitive political topics, and they are undoubtedly matters of profound " 'value and concern to the public.' " *Snyder v. Phelps*, 562 U.S. 443, 453, 131 S.Ct. 1207, 179 L.Ed.2d 172 (2011). We have often recognized that such speech " 'occupies the highest rung of the hierarchy of First Amendment values' " and merits " 'special protection.' ". . .

The only remaining question under *Pickering* is whether the State's proffered interests justify the heavy burden that agency fees inflict on nonmembers' First Amendment interests. Although the dissent would accept without any serious independent evaluation the State's assertion that the absence of agency fees would cripple public-sector unions and thus impair the efficiency of government operations, ample experience, as we have noted, shows that this is questionable. Especially in light of the more rigorous form of Pickering analysis that would apply in this context, the balance tips decisively in favor of the employees' free speech rights.[23]

---

[23] Claiming that our decision will hobble government operations, the dissent asserts that it would prevent a government employer from taking action against disruptive non-unionized employees in two carefully constructed hypothetical situations. Both hypotheticals are short on potentially important details, but in any event, neither would be affected by our decision in this case. Rather, both would simply call for the application of the standard Pickering test. In one of the hypotheticals, teachers "protest merit pay in the school cafeteria." If such a case actually arose, it would be important to know, among other things, whether the teachers involved were supposed to be teaching in their classrooms at the time in question and whether the protest occurred in the presence of students during the student lunch period. If both those conditions were met, the teachers would presumably be violating content-neutral rules regarding their duty to teach at specified times and places, and their conduct might well have a disruptive effect on the educational process. Thus, in the dissent's hypothetical, the school's interests might well outweigh those of the teachers, but in this hypothetical case, as in all Pickering cases, the particular facts would be very important. In the other hypothetical, employees agitate for a better health plan "at various inopportune times and places." Here, the lack of factual detail makes it impossible to evaluate how the Pickering balance would come out. The term "agitat[ion]" can encompass a wide range of conduct, as well as speech. And the time and place of the agitation would also be important.

We readily acknowledge, as *Pickering* did, that "the State has interests as an employer in regulating the speech of its employees that differ significantly from those it possesses in connection with regulation of the speech of the citizenry in general." It is also not disputed that the State may require that a union serve as exclusive bargaining agent for its employees—itself a significant impingement on associational freedoms that would not be tolerated in other contexts. We simply draw the line at allowing the government to go further still and require all employees to support the union irrespective of whether they share its views.

VI

There remains the question whether *stare decisis* nonetheless counsels against overruling *Abood*. It does not. . . .

Abood went wrong at the start when it concluded that two prior decisions, *Railway Employes v. Hanson*, 351 U.S. 225, 76 S.Ct. 714, 100 L.Ed. 1112 (1956), and *Machinists v. Street*, 367 U.S. 740, 81 S.Ct. 1784, 6 L.Ed.2d 1141 (1961), "appear[ed] to require validation of the agency-shop agreement before [the Court]." 431 U.S., at 226, 97 S.Ct. 1782. Properly understood, those decisions did no such thing. Both cases involved Congress's "bare authorization" of private-sector union shops under the Railway Labor Act. *Abood* failed to appreciate that a very different First Amendment question arises when a State requires its employees to pay agency fees. *Abood*'s unwarranted reliance on *Hanson* and *Street* appears to have contributed to another mistake: *Abood* judged the constitutionality of public-sector agency fees under a deferential standard that finds no support in our free speech cases. *Abood* did not independently evaluate the strength of the government interests that were said to support the challenged agency-fee provision; nor did it ask how well that provision actually promoted those interests or whether they could have been adequately served without impinging so heavily on the free speech rights of nonmembers. *Abood* also did not sufficiently take into account the difference between the effects of agency fees in public- and private-sector collective bargaining. "In the public sector, core issues such as wages, pensions, and benefits are important political issues, but that is generally not so in the private sector." *Harris,* 134 S.Ct., at 2632. . . .

Another relevant consideration in the *stare decisis* calculus is the workability of the precedent in question. *Abood*'s line between chargeable and nonchargeable union expenditures has proved to be impossible to draw with precision. Respondents agree that *Abood*'s chargeable-nonchargeable line suffers from "a vagueness problem," that it sometimes "allows what it shouldn't allow," and that "a firm[er] line c[ould] be drawn. . . . This concession only underscores the reality that *Abood* has proved unworkable: Not even the parties defending agency fees support the line that it has taken this Court over 40 years to draw. . . . Objecting employees also face a daunting and expensive task if they wish to challenge union chargeability determinations. . . .

Developments since *Abood,* both factual and legal, have also "eroded" the decision's "underpinnings" and left it an outlier among our First Amendment cases. *Abood* pinned its result on the "unsupported empirical assumption" that "the principle of exclusive representation in the public sector is dependent on a union or agency shop." *Harris,* 134 S.Ct., at 2634; *Abood,* 97 S.Ct. 1782. But, as already noted, experience has shown otherwise. It is also significant that the Court decided *Abood* against a very different legal and economic backdrop. Public-sector unionism was a relatively new phenomenon in 1977. Since then, public-sector union membership has come to surpass private-sector union membership, even though there are nearly four times as many total private-sector employees as public-sector employees. These developments, and the political debate over public spending and debt they have spurred, have given collective-bargaining issues a political valence that *Abood* did not fully appreciate.

Abood is also an "anomaly" in our First Amendment jurisprudence, as we recognized in *Harris* and *Knox. Abood* particularly sticks out when viewed against our cases holding that public employees generally may not be required to support a political party. It is an odd feature of our First Amendment cases that political patronage has been deemed largely unconstitutional, while forced subsidization of union speech (which has no such pedigree) has been largely permitted.

In some cases, reliance provides a strong reason for adhering to established law, and this is the factor that is stressed most strongly by respondents, their *amici,* and the dissent. They contend that collective-bargaining agreements now in effect were negotiated with agency fees in mind and that unions may have given up other benefits in exchange for provisions granting them such fees. In this case, however, reliance does not carry decisive weight. For one thing, it would be unconscionable to permit free speech rights to be abridged in perpetuity in order to preserve contract provisions that will expire on their own in a few years' time. For another, *Abood* does not provide "a clear or easily applicable standard, so arguments for reliance based on its clarity are misplaced. This is especially so because public-sector unions have been on notice for years regarding this Court's misgivings about *Abood.* In short, the uncertain status of *Abood,* the lack of clarity it provides, the short-term nature of collective-bargaining agreements, and the ability of unions to protect themselves if an agency-fee provision was crucial to its bargain all work to undermine the force of reliance as a factor supporting *Abood.* . . .

We recognize that the loss of payments from nonmembers may cause unions to experience unpleasant transition costs in the short term, and may require unions to make adjustments in order to attract and retain members. But we must weigh these disadvantages against the considerable windfall that unions have received under *Abood* for the past 41 years. It is hard to estimate how many billions of dollars have been taken from nonmembers and transferred to public-sector unions in violation of the First Amendment. Those unconstitutional exactions cannot be allowed to continue indefinitely. . . .

Abood was wrongly decided and is now overruled. The judgment of the United States Court of Appeals for the Seventh Circuit is reversed, and the case is remanded for further proceedings consistent with this opinion.

It is so ordered.

JUSTICE KAGAN, with whom GINSBURG, BREYER, & SOTOMAYOR JJ., join, dissenting.

For over 40 years, *Abood v. Detroit Bd. of Ed.* struck a stable balance between public employees' First Amendment rights and government entities' interests in running their workforces as they thought proper. Under that decision, a government entity could require public employees to pay a fair share of the cost that a union incurs when negotiating on their behalf over terms of employment. That holding fit comfortably with this Court's general framework for evaluating claims that a condition of public employment violates the First Amendment. The Court's decisions have long made plain that government entities have substantial latitude to regulate their employees' speech—especially about terms of employment—in the interest of operating their workplaces effectively.

Not any longer. Today, the Court succeeds in its 6-year campaign to reverse *Abood*. Rarely if ever has the Court overruled a decision—let alone one of this import—with so little regard for the usual principles of *stare decisis*. There are no special justifications for reversing *Abood*. It has proved workable. No recent developments have eroded its underpinnings. And it is deeply entrenched, in both the law and the real world. More than 20 States have statutory schemes built on the decision. Those laws underpin thousands of ongoing contracts involving millions of employees. Reliance interests do not come any stronger than those surrounding *Abood*. And likewise, judicial disruption does not get any greater than what the Court does today. I respectfully dissent.

[*Abood*] involved a union that had been certified as the exclusive representative of Detroit's public school teachers. The union's collective-bargaining agreement with the city included an "agency shop" clause, which required teachers who had not joined the union to pay it "a service charge equal to the regular dues required of [u]nion members." A group of non-union members sued over that clause, arguing that it violated the First Amendment. In considering their challenge, the Court canvassed the purposes of the "agency shop" clause. It was rooted, the Court understood, in the "principle of exclusive union representation"—a "central element" in "industrial relations" since the New Deal. But for an exclusive-bargaining arrangement to work, such an employer often thought, the union needed adequate funding. And there is no way to confine the union's services to union members alone (and thus to trim costs) because unions must by law fairly represent all employees in a given bargaining unit—union members and non-members alike. But the Court acknowledged as well the "First Amendment interests" of dissenting employees. It recognized that some workers might oppose positions the union takes in collective bargaining, or even "unionism itself." And still more, it understood that unions often advance "political and ideological" views outside the collective-bargaining context—as when they "contribute to political candidates." Employees might well object to the use of their money to support such "ideological causes." So the Court struck a balance, which has governed this area ever since. On the one hand, employees could be required to pay fees to support the union in "collective bargaining, contract administration, and grievance adjustment." There, the Court held, the "important government interests" in having a stably funded bargaining partner justify "the impingement upon" public employees' expression. But on the other hand, employees could not be compelled to fund the union's political and ideological activities. Outside the collective-bargaining sphere, the Court determined, an employee's First Amendment rights defeated any conflicting government interest.

And the balance *Abood* struck between public employers' interests and public employees' expression is right at home in First Amendment doctrine. *Abood*'s reasoning about governmental interests has three connected parts. First, exclusive representation arrangements benefit some government entities because they can facilitate stable labor relations. In particular, such arrangements eliminate the potential for inter-union conflict and streamline the process of negotiating terms of employment. Second, the government may be unable to avail itself of those benefits unless the single union has a secure source of funding. The various tasks involved in representing employees cost money; if the union doesn't have enough, it can't be an effective employee representative and bargaining partner. And third, agency fees are often needed to ensure such stable funding. That is because without those fees, employees have every incentive to free ride on the union dues paid by others. The majority stakes everything on the third point—the conclusion that maintaining an effective system of exclusive representation often entails agency fees (It "is simply not true" that exclusive representation and agency fees are "inextricably linked"). But basic economic theory shows why a government would think that agency fees are necessary for exclusive representation to work. What ties the two together, as *Abood* recognized, is the likelihood of free-riding when fees are absent. Remember that once a union achieves exclusive-representation status, the law compels it to fairly represent all workers in the bargaining unit, whether or not they join or contribute to the union. Because of that legal duty, the union cannot give special advantages to its own members. And that in turn creates a collective action problem of nightmarish proportions. Everyone—not just those who oppose the union, but also those who back it—has an economic incentive to withhold dues; only altruism or loyalty— as against financial self-interest—can explain why an employee would pay the union for its services. And so emerged *Abood*'s rule allowing fair-share agreements: That rule ensured that a union would receive sufficient funds, despite its legally imposed disability, to effectively carry out its duties as exclusive representative of the government's employees.

The majority's initial response to this reasoning is simply to dismiss it. "Many private groups speak out" in ways that will "benefit nonmembers." But that disregards the defining characteristic of this free-rider argument—that unions, unlike those many other private groups, must serve members and non-members alike. Groups advocating for "senior citizens or veterans" (to use the majority's examples) have no legal duty to provide benefits to all those individuals: They can spur people to pay dues by conferring all kinds of special advantages on their dues-paying members. Unions are—by law—in a different position, as this Court has long recognized. Justice Scalia, responding to the same argument as the majority's, may have put the point best. In a way that is true of no other private group, the "law requires the union to carry" non-members—"indeed, requires the union to go out of its way to benefit [them], even at the expense of its other interests." *Lehnert v. Ferris Faculty Assn.*, 500 U.S. 507, 556, 111 S.Ct. 1950, 114 L.Ed.2d 572 (1991) (opinion concurring in part and dissenting in part). That special feature was what justified *Abood*: "Where the state imposes upon the union a duty to deliver services, it may permit the union to demand reimbursement for them." 500 U.S., at 556.

The majority's fallback argument purports to respond to the distinctive position of unions, but still misses *Abood*'s economic insight. Here, the majority delivers a four-page exegesis on why unions will seek to serve as an exclusive bargaining representative even "if they are not given agency fees." But that response avoids the key question, which is whether unions without agency fees will be able to (not whether they will want to) carry on as an effective exclusive representative. And as to that question, the majority again fails to reckon with how economically rational actors behave—in public as well as private workplaces. Without a fair-share agreement, the class of union non-members spirals upward.

Employees (including those who love the union) realize that they can get the same benefits even if they let their memberships expire. And as more and more stop paying dues, those left must take up the financial slack (and anyway, begin to feel like suckers)—so they too quit the union. The result is to frustrate the interests of every government entity that thinks a strong exclusive-representation scheme will promote stable labor relations. . . .

In many cases over many decades, this Court has addressed how the First Amendment applies when the government, acting not as sovereign but as employer, limits its workers' speech. Those decisions have granted substantial latitude to the government, in recognition of its significant interests in managing its workforce so as to best serve the public. *Abood* fit neatly with that caselaw, in both reasoning and result. Indeed, its reversal today creates a significant anomaly—an exception, applying to union fees alone, from the usual rules governing public employees' speech. . . . In striking the proper balance between employee speech rights and managerial interests, the Court has long applied a test originating in *Pickering v. Board of Ed. of Township High School Dist. 205, Will Cty.* That case arose out of an individual employment action: the firing of a public school teacher. As we later described the *Pickering* inquiry, the Court first asks whether the employee "spoke as a citizen on a matter of public concern." If she did not—but rather spoke as an employee on a workplace matter—she has no "possibility of a First Amendment claim": A public employer can curtail her speech just as a private one could. Ibid. But if she did speak as a citizen on a public matter, the public employer must demonstrate "an adequate justification for treating the employee differently from any other member of the general public." The government, that is, needs to show that legitimate workplace interests lay behind the speech regulation.

Abood coheres with that framework. . . . *Abood* and *Pickering* raised variants of the same basic issue: the extent of the government's authority to make employment decisions affecting expression. And in both, the Court struck the same basic balance, enabling the government to curb speech when—but only when—the regulation was designed to protect its managerial interests. Consider the parallels: *Abood* allowed the government to mandate fees for collective bargaining—just as *Pickering* permits the government to regulate employees' speech on similar workplace matters. But still, *Abood* realized that compulsion could go too far. The Court barred the use of fees for union speech supporting political candidates or "ideological causes." That speech, it understood, was "unrelated to [the union's] duties as exclusive bargaining representative," but instead was directed at the broader public sphere. And for that reason, the Court saw no legitimate managerial interests in compelling its subsidization. The employees' First Amendment claims would thus prevail—as, again, they would have under *Pickering*.

Abood thus dovetailed with the Court's usual attitude in First Amendment cases toward the regulation of public employees' speech. That attitude is one of respect—even solicitude—for the government's prerogatives as an employer. So long as the government is acting as an employer—rather than exploiting the employment relationship for other ends—it has a wide berth, comparable to that of a private employer. And when the regulated expression concerns the terms and conditions of employment—the very stuff of the employment relationship—the government really cannot lose. There, managerial interests are obvious and strong. And so government employees are . . . just employees, even though they work for the government. Except that today the government does lose, in a first for the law. Now, the government can constitutionally adopt all policies regulating core workplace speech in pursuit of managerial goals—save this single one. . . .

[T]he majority's distinction between compelling and restricting speech lacks force. The majority posits that compelling speech always works a greater injury, and so always requires a greater justification. But the only case the majority cites for that reading of our precedent is possibly (thankfully) the most exceptional in our First Amendment annals: It involved the state forcing children to swear an oath contrary to their religious beliefs. (quoting *West Virginia Bd. of Ed. v. Barnette*). Regulations challenged as compelling expression do not usually look anything like that—and for that reason, the standard First Amendment rule is that the "difference between compelled speech and compelled silence" is "without constitutional significance." *Riley v. National Federation of Blind of N. C., Inc.*, 487 U.S. 781, 796, 108 S.Ct. 2667, 101 L.Ed.2d 669 (1988); see *Wooley v. Maynard*, 430 U.S. 705, 714, 97 S.Ct. 1428, 51 L.Ed.2d 752 (1977) (referring to "[t]he right to speak and the right to refrain from speaking" as "complementary components" of the First Amendment). And if anything, the First Amendment scales tip the opposite way when (as here) the government is not compelling actual speech, but instead compelling a subsidy that others will use for expression.[3]

[S]peech about the terms and conditions of employment—the essential stuff of collective bargaining—has never survived Pickering's first step. This Court has rejected all attempts by employees to make a

---

[3]   That's why this Court has blessed the constitutionality of compelled speech subsidies in a variety of cases beyond *Abood*, involving a variety of contexts beyond labor relations. The list includes mandatory fees imposed on state bar members (for professional expression); university students (for campus events); and fruit processors (for generic advertising). See *Keller v. State Bar of Cal.*, 496 U.S. 1, 14, 110 S.Ct. 2228, 110 L.Ed.2d 1 (1990); *Board of Regents of Univ. of Wis. System v. Southworth*, 529 U.S. 217, 233, 120 S.Ct. 1346, 146 L.Ed.2d 193 (2000); *Glickman v. Wileman Brothers & Elliott, Inc.*, 521 U.S. 457, 474, 117 S.Ct. 2130, 138 L.Ed.2d 585 (1997).

"federal constitutional issue" out of basic "employment matters, including working conditions, pay, discipline, promotions, leave, vacations, and terminations." Consider an analogy, not involving union fees: Suppose a government entity disciplines a group of (non-unionized) employees for agitating for a better health plan at various inopportune times and places. The better health plan will of course drive up public spending; so according to the majority's analysis, the employees' speech satisfies Pickering's "public concern" test. Or similarly, suppose a public employer penalizes a group of (non-unionized) teachers who protest merit pay in the school cafeteria. Once again, the majority's logic runs, the speech is of "public concern," so the employees have a plausible First Amendment claim. (And indeed, the majority appears to concede as much, by asserting that the results in these hypotheticals should turn on various "factual detail[s]" relevant to the interest balancing that occurs at the Pickering test's second step. But in fact, this Court has always understood such cases to end at Pickering's first step: If an employee's speech is about, in, and directed to the workplace, she has no "possibility of a First Amendment claim." *Garcetti*, 547 U.S., at 418. So take your pick. Either the majority is exposing government entities across the country to increased First Amendment litigation and liability—and thus preventing them from regulating their workforces as private employers could. Or else, when actual cases of this kind come around, we will discover that today's majority has crafted a "unions only" carve-out to our employee-speech law. . .

The key point about *Abood* is that it fit naturally with this Court's consistent teaching about the permissibility of regulating public employees' speech. The Court allows a government entity to regulate that expression in aid of managing its workforce to effectively provide public services. That is just what a government aims to do when it enforces a fair-share agreement. And so, the key point about today's decision is that it creates an unjustified hole in the law, applicable to union fees alone. This case is sui generis among those addressing public employee speech—and will almost surely remain so.

But the worse part of today's opinion is where the majority subverts all known principles of *stare decisis*. The majority makes plain, in the first 33 pages of its decision, that it believes *Abood* was wrong. But even if that were true (which it is not), it is not enough. "Respecting *stare decisis* means sticking to some wrong decisions." *Kimble v. Marvel Entertainment, LLC,* 135 S.Ct. 2401, 2409, 192 L.Ed.2d 463 (2015). Any departure from settled precedent (so the Court has often stated) demands a "special justification—over and above the belief that the precedent was wrongly decided." 135 S.Ct., at 2409 see, e.g., *Arizona v. Rumsey*, 104 S.Ct. 2305, 81 L.Ed.2d 164 (1984). And the majority does not have anything close. To the contrary: all that is "special" in this case—

especially the massive reliance interests at stake—demands retaining *Abood*, beyond even the normal precedent. And *Abood* is not just any precedent: It is embedded in the law (not to mention, as I'll later address, in the world) in a way not many decisions are. Over four decades, this Court has cited *Abood* favorably many times, and has affirmed and applied its central distinction between the costs of collective bargaining (which the government can charge to all employees) and those of political activities (which it cannot). And indeed, the Court has relied on that rule when deciding cases involving compelled speech subsidies outside the labor sphere—cases today's decision does not question. See, e.g., *Keller v. State Bar of Cal.*, 496 U.S. 1, 9–17, 110 S.Ct. 2228, 110 L.Ed.2d 1 (1990) (state bar fees); *Board of Regents of Univ. of Wis. System v. Southworth*, 529 U.S. 217, 230–232, 120 S.Ct. 1346, 146 L.Ed.2d 193 (2000) (public university student fees); *Glickman v. Wileman Brothers & Elliott, Inc.*, 521 U.S. 457, 471–473, 117 S.Ct. 2130, 138 L.Ed.2d 585 (1997) (commercial advertising assessments).

Ignoring our repeated validation of *Abood*, the majority claims it has become "an outlier among our First Amendment cases." That claim fails most spectacularly for reasons already discussed: *Abood* coheres with the *Pickering* approach to reviewing regulation of public employees' speech. Needing to stretch further, the majority suggests that *Abood* conflicts with "our political patronage decisions." But in fact those decisions strike a balance much like *Abood*'s. On the one hand, the Court has enabled governments to compel policymakers to support a political party, because that requirement (like fees for collective bargaining) can reasonably be thought to advance the interest in workplace effectiveness. See *Elrod v. Burns*, 427 U.S. 347, 366–367, 96 S.Ct. 2673, 49 L.Ed.2d 547 (1976); *Branti v. Finkel*, 445 U.S. 507, 517, 100 S.Ct. 1287, 63 L.Ed.2d 574 (1980). On the other hand, the Court has barred governments from extending that rule to non-policymaking employees because that application (like fees for political campaigns) can't be thought to promote that interest, see *Elrod*, 427 U.S., at 366, 96 S.Ct. 2673; the government is instead trying to "leverage the employment relationship" to achieve other goals, *Garcetti*, 547 U.S., at 419, 126 S.Ct. 1951. So all that the majority has left is *Knox* and *Harris*. Dicta in those recent decisions indeed began the assault on *Abood* that has culminated today. But neither actually addressed the extent to which a public employer may regulate its own employees' speech. Relying on them is bootstrapping—and mocking *stare decisis*. Don't like a decision? Just throw some gratuitous criticisms into a couple of opinions and a few years later point to them as "special justifications."

The majority is likewise wrong to invoke "workability" as a reason for overruling *Abood*. Does *Abood* require drawing a line? Yes, between a union's collective-bargaining activities and its political activities. Is that line perfectly and pristinely "precis[e]," as the majority demands? Well, not quite that—but as exercises of constitutional linedrawing go, *Abood* stands well above average. As I wrote in *Harris* a few Terms ago: "If the kind of hand-wringing about blurry lines that the majority offers were enough to justify breaking with precedent, we might have to discard whole volumes of the U.S. Reports." 134 S.Ct., at 2652. . . .

And in any event, one *stare decisis* factor—reliance—dominates all others here and demands keeping *Abood*. *Stare decisis*, this Court has held, "has added force when the legislature, in the public sphere, and citizens, in the private realm, have acted in reliance on a previous decision." *Hilton v. South Carolina Public Railways Comm'n*, 502 U.S. 197, 202, 112 S.Ct. 560, 116 L.Ed.2d 560 (1991). That is because overruling a decision would then "require an extensive legislative response" or "dislodge settled rights and expectations." Both will happen here: The Court today wreaks havoc on entrenched legislative and contractual arrangements. Over 20 States have by now enacted statutes authorizing fair-share provisions. To be precise, 22 States, the District of Columbia, and Puerto Rico—plus another two States for police and firefighter unions. Many of those States have multiple statutory provisions, with variations for different categories of public employees. Every one of them will now need to come up with new ways—elaborated in new statutes—to structure relations between government employers and their workers. The majority responds, in a footnote no less, that this is of no proper concern to the Court. But in fact, we have weighed heavily against "abandon[ing] our settled jurisprudence" that "[s]tate legislatures have relied upon" it and would have to "reexamine [and amend] their statutes" if it were overruled. *Allied-Signal, Inc. v. Director, Div. of Taxation,* 504 U.S. 768, 785, 112 S.Ct. 2251, 119 L.Ed.2d 533 (1992); *Hilton,* 502 U.S., at 203, 112 S.Ct. 560. Still more, thousands of current contracts covering millions of workers provide for agency fees. Usually, this Court recognizes that "[c]onsiderations in favor of stare decisis are at their acme in cases involving property and contract rights." *Payne,* 501 U.S., at 828, 111 S.Ct. 2597. Not today. The majority undoes bargains reached all over the country. It prevents the parties from fulfilling other commitments they have made based on those agreements. It forces the parties—immediately—to renegotiate once-settled terms and create new tradeoffs. It does so knowing that many of the parties will have to revise (or redo) multiple contracts simultaneously. (New York City, for example, has agreed to agency fees in 144 contracts with 97 public-sector unions). It does so knowing that those renegotiations will occur in an environment of legal uncertainty, as state governments scramble to enact new labor legislation. It does so with no real clue of what will happen next—of how its action will alter public-sector labor relations. It does so even though the government services affected—policing, firefighting, teaching, transportation, sanitation (and more)—affect the quality of life of tens of millions of Americans. . . .

The majority, though, offers another reason for not worrying about reliance: The parties, it says, "have been on notice for years regarding this Court's misgivings *about Abood.*" But that argument reflects a radically wrong understanding of how stare decisis operates. Justice Scalia once confronted a similar argument for "disregard[ing] reliance interests" and showed how antithetical it was to rule-of-law principles. *Quill Corp. v. North Dakota,* 504 U.S. 298, 320, 112 S.Ct. 1904, 119 L.Ed.2d 91 (1992) (concurring opinion). He noted first what we always tell lower courts: "If a precedent of this Court has direct application in a case, yet appears to rest on reasons rejected in some other line of decisions, [they] should follow the case which directly controls, leaving to this Court the prerogative of overruling its own decisions." Id., at 321, 112 S.Ct. 1904 (quoting *Rodriguez de Quijas v. Shearson/American Express, Inc.,* 490 U.S. 477, 484, 109 S.Ct. 1917, 104 L.Ed.2d 526 (1989); some alterations omitted). That instruction, Justice Scalia explained, was "incompatible" with an expectation that "private parties anticipate our overrulings." 504 U.S., at 320, 112 S.Ct. 1904. He concluded: "[R]eliance upon a square, unabandoned holding of the Supreme Court is always justifiable reliance." Ibid. Abood's holding was square. It was unabandoned before today. It was, in other words, the law—however much some were working overtime to make it not. Parties, both unions and governments, were thus justified in relying on it. And they did rely, to an extent rare among our decisions. To dismiss the overthrowing of their settled expectations as entailing no more than some "adjustments" and "unpleasant transition costs," is to trivialize *stare decisis.*

There is no sugarcoating today's opinion. The majority overthrows a decision entrenched in this Nation's law—and in its economic life—for over 40 years. As a result, it prevents the American people, acting through their state and local officials, from making important choices about workplace governance. And it does so by weaponizing the First Amendment, in a way that unleashes judges, now and in the future, to intervene in economic and regulatory policy. In contrast to the vigor of its attack on *Abood,* the majority's discussion of *stare decisis* barely limps to the finish line. And no wonder: The standard factors this Court considers when deciding to overrule a decision all cut one way. *Abood*'s legal underpinnings have not eroded over time: *Abood* is now, as it was when issued, consistent with this Court's First Amendment law. *Abood* provided a workable standard for courts to apply. And *Abood* has generated enormous reliance interests. The majority has overruled *Abood* for no exceptional or special reason, but because it never liked the decision. It has overruled *Abood* because it wanted to. Because, that is, it wanted to pick the winning side in what should be—and until now, has been—an energetic policy debate. . .

And maybe most alarming, the majority has chosen the winners by turning the First Amendment into a sword, and using it against workaday economic and regulatory policy. Today is not the first time the Court has wielded the First Amendment in such an aggressive way. See, e.g., *National Institute of Family and Life Advocates v. Becerra*, 138 S.Ct. 2361, 138 L.Ed.2d 2361, 2018 WL 3116336 (2018) (invalidating a law requiring medical and counseling facilities to provide relevant information to users); *Sorrell v. IMS Health Inc.*, 564 U.S. 552, 131 S.Ct. 2653, 180 L.Ed.2d 544 (2011) (striking down a law that restricted pharmacies from selling various data). And it threatens not to be the last. Speech is everywhere—a part of every human activity (employment, health care, securities trading, you name it). For that reason, almost all economic and regulatory policy affects or touches speech. So the majority's road runs long. And at every stop are black-robed rulers overriding citizens' choices. The First Amendment was meant for better things. It was meant not to undermine but to protect democratic governance—including over the role of public-sector unions.

NOTES

Citing *West Virginia Bd. of Ed. v. Barnette,* the majority states that "measures compelling speech are at least as threatening" as regulations restricting speech, and that "when speech is compelled, additional damage is done" because in that situation, "individuals are coerced into betraying their convictions." *Barnette* struck down a flag salute law that required all students, regardless of their religious beliefs, to salute the American flag. According to the majority, *Barnette* stands for the principle that "a law commanding 'involuntary affirmation' of objected-to beliefs would require 'even more immediate and urgent grounds' than a law demanding silence." Are there principled differences under the First Amendment between government restricting speech and government compelling speech? Is *Barnette* an apt precedent for a state law that requires an employee to pay union dues for the union's collective bargaining activities but who is exempted from paying a portion of the dues that relate to the union's political activities? The majority states that "compelling a person to *subsidize* the speech of others" raises First Amendment concerns. However, the majority neither cited nor discussed the several decisions in which the Court upheld compelled speech subsidies: *Keller v. State Bar of California* (state bar fees); *Board of Regents of Univ. of Wis. System v. Southworth* (public university student fees); *Glickman v. Wileman Brothers & Elliot, Inc.* (commercial advertising fees). Are these cases distinguishable from *Abood*?

10–11   CAMPAIGN SPEECH AND FINANCING

Unabridged, p. 1264; add to Note 5, after *Republican Party of Minnesota v. White*:

Abridged, p. 974; add to Note 4, after *Republican Party of Minnesota v. White*:

The Florida Supreme Court adopted Canon 7C(1) of its Code of Judicial Conduct (corresponding to ABA Model Judicial Code, Rule 4.1(A)(8), which provides that judicial candidates "shall not personally solicit campaign funds . . . but may establish committees of responsible persons" to raise money for election campaigns. Chief Justice Roberts, for a fractured Court (5 to 4), held that Florida has a compelling interest in "preserving the public confidence in the integrity of its judiciary" and that this prohibition on personal solicitation is narrowly tailored to avoid unnecessarily abridging speech. *Williams-Yulee v. Florida Bar*, 575 U.S. ___, 135 S.Ct. 1656, 191 L.Ed.2d 570 (2015). This is "one of the rare cases in which a speech restriction withstands strict scrutiny." The Florida (and the ABA) Rule require judges and judicial candidates to direct campaign committees to solicit contributions. While personal solicitation and committee solicitation might operate the same in substance, "a State may conclude that they present markedly different appearances to the public."

Williams-Yulee drafted a letter announcing her candidacy for judicial office and in that letter asked for contributions to her political campaign. She also posted the letter online. She lost the primary and the Florida Bar filed a complaint against her for violating the solicitation rule. The Florida Supreme Court upheld a public reprimand of Ms. Williams-Yulee. The Rule provides that the judicial candidate "shall not personally solicit campaign funds." Williams-Yulee agreed that the State could forbid face-to-face solicitation but she never engaged in any face-to-face solicitation. She never walked up to a contributor who handed her a $100 bill. Instead, she wrote a letter, signed it, mailed it to local voters, and posted it on her website. Her actions violated this Rule, which required her to set up a committee to solicit the funds.

Scalia, J., filed a dissenting opinion, which Thomas, J., joined. Kennedy & Alito, JJ, also filed dissenting opinions. The Florida Rule specifically permits judicial candidates to write thank you notes to campaign donors, so candidates know who contributed and who did not. This Rule also does not ban judicial candidates from personally asking individuals for personal gifts or loans as long as the gift or loan is not a campaign contribution—that is, the donor did not give it for the purpose of influencing the results of an election. Williams-Yulee may not write a letter asking for campaign contribution from her parents who have no chance of appearing in her court. Yet, the Rule allows her personally to solicit donations to help her fight the Florida Bar's charges.

10–12 OBSCENITY

10–12.3 THE INTERNET

Unabridged, p. 1323; add to *Notes*:

Packingham v. North Carolina, 582 U.S. ___, 137 S.Ct. 1730, 198 L.Ed.2d 273 (2017). A North Carolina statute makes it a felony for a registered sex offender "to access a commercial social networking Web site where the sex offender knows that the site permits minor children to become members or to create or maintain personal Web pages." Packingham was convicted of posting a statement on his personal Facebook profile about a positive experience in traffic court. The trial court gave him a suspended sentence.

Kennedy, J., (joined by Ginsburg, Breyer, Sotomayor, and Kagan; Gorsuch did not participate), held that North Carolina's law violates free speech clause. He cautioned, "The forces and directions of the Internet are so new, so protean, and so far reaching that courts must be conscious that what they say today might be obsolete tomorrow." Hence, "the Court must exercise extreme caution before suggesting that the First Amendment provides scant protection for access to vast networks in that medium."

Even if that this law is content neutral and subject to intermediate scrutiny, it is not narrowly tailored to serve a significant governmental interest. It applies to social networking sites like Facebook, LinkedIn, and Twitter. The Court assumed that, under the First Amendment, a state may enact specific, narrowly-tailored laws that prohibit a sex offender from engaging in conduct that often presages a sexual crime, like contacting a minor or using a website to gather information about a minor. The problem is that North Carolina prohibited much more, and could not show that its "sweeping law" was necessary to keep sex offenders away from minors:

> "North Carolina with one broad stroke bars access to what for many are the principal sources for knowing current events, checking ads for employment, speaking and listening in the modern public square, and otherwise exploring the vast realms of human thought and knowledge. These websites can provide perhaps the most powerful mechanisms available to a private citizen to make his or her voice heard. They allow a person with an Internet connection to 'become a town crier with a voice that resonates farther than it could from any soapbox.' "

Alito, J., concurred in the judgment, joined by Roberts, C.J., and Thomas, J., criticizing the majority for its "undisciplined dicta," and its inability "to resist musings that seem to equate the entirety of the internet with public streets and parks."

CHAPTER 11

RELIGION

■ ■ ■

11–2 NONFINANCIAL ASSISTANCE TO RELIGION

11–2.2 THE PUBLIC FORUM AND THE ESTABLISHMENT CLAUSE

Unabridged, p. 1411; at end of *Notes*, add new case:

AMERICAN LEGION, ET AL. V. AMERICAN HUMANIST ASSN., ET AL.

139 S.Ct. 2067, ___ L.Ed.2d ___ (2019).

JUSTICE ALITO delivered the opinion of the Court:

Since 1925, the Bladensburg Peace Cross (Cross) has stood as a tribute to 49 area soldiers who gave their lives in the First World War. Eighty-nine years after the dedication of the Cross, respondents filed this lawsuit, claiming that they are offended by the sight of the memorial on public land and that its presence there and the expenditure of public funds to maintain it violate the Establishment Clause of the First Amendment. To remedy this violation, they asked a federal court to order the relocation or demolition of the Cross or at least the removal of its arms. The Court of Appeals for the Fourth Circuit agreed that the memorial is unconstitutional and remanded for a determination of the proper remedy. We now reverse. . . .

The cross came into widespread use as a symbol of Christianity by the fourth century, and it retains that meaning today. But there are many contexts in which the symbol has also taken on a secular meaning. Indeed, there are instances in which its message is now almost entirely secular. A cross appears as part of many registered trademarks held by businesses and secular organizations, including Blue Cross Blue Shield, the Bayer Group, and some Johnson & Johnson products. Many of these marks relate to health care, and it is likely that the association of the cross with healing had a religious origin. But the current use of these marks is indisputably secular. . . .

The image used in the Bladensburg memorial—a plain Latin cross—also took on new meaning after World War I. The image of a simple white cross developed into a central symbol of the conflict. Perhaps most famously, John McCrae's poem, In Flanders Fields, began with these memorable lines:

"In Flanders fields the poppies blow

Between the crosses, row on row."

. . .Recognition of the cross's symbolism extended to local communities across the country. In late 1918, residents of Prince George's County, Maryland, formed a committee for the purpose of erecting a memorial for the county's fallen soldiers. Although we do not know precisely why the committee chose the cross, it is unsurprising that the committee—and many others commemorating World War I—adopted a symbol so widely associated with that wrenching event. The Cross was to stand at the terminus of another World War I memorial—the National Defense Highway, which connects Washington to Annapolis. . . .

By 1922, however, the committee had run out of funds, and progress on the Cross had stalled. The local post of the American Legion took over the project, and the monument was finished in 1925. The completed monument is a 32-foot tall Latin cross that sits on a large pedestal. The American Legion's emblem is displayed at its center, and the words "Valor," "Endurance," "Courage," and "Devotion" are inscribed at its base, one on each of the four faces. The pedestal also features a 9- by 2.5-foot bronze plaque explaining that the monument is "Dedicated to the heroes of Prince George's County, Maryland who lost their lives in the Great War for the liberty of the world." The plaque lists the names of 49 local men, both Black and White, who died in the war. The Cross has served as the site of patriotic events honoring veterans, including gatherings on Veterans Day, Memorial Day, and Independence Day. Like the dedication itself, these events have typically included an invocation, a keynote speaker, and a benediction. . . .

As the area around the Cross developed, the monument came to be at the center of a busy intersection. In 1961, the Maryland-National Capital Park and Planning Commission (Commission) acquired the Cross and the land on which it sits in order to preserve the monument and address traffic-safety concerns. The American Legion reserved the right to continue using the memorial to host a variety of ceremonies, including events in memory of departed veterans. Over the next five decades, the Commission spent approximately $ 117,000 to maintain and preserve the monument. In 2008, it budgeted an additional $ 100,000 for renovations and repairs to the Cross.

In 2012, nearly 90 years after the Cross was dedicated and more than 50 years after the Commission acquired it, the American Humanist Association (AHA) lodged a complaint with the Commission. The complaint alleged that the Cross's presence on public land and the

Commission's maintenance of the memorial violate the Establishment Clause of the First Amendment. The AHA sought declaratory and injunctive relief requiring "removal or demolition of the Cross, or removal of the arms from the Cross to form a non-religious slab or obelisk." The American Legion intervened to defend the Cross.

The District Court granted summary judgment for the Commission and the American Legion. The Cross, the District Court held, satisfies both the three-pronged test announced in *Lemon v. Kurtzman,* and the analysis applied by Justice BREYER in upholding the Ten Commandments monument at issue in *Van Orden v. Perry.* Applying that test, the District Court determined that the Commission had secular purposes for acquiring and maintaining the Cross—namely, to commemorate World War I and to ensure traffic safety. The court also found that a reasonable observer aware of the Cross's history, setting, and secular elements "would not view the Monument as having the effect of impermissibly endorsing religion." Nor, according to the court, did the Commission's maintenance of the memorial create the kind of "continued and repeated government involvement with religion" that would constitute an excessive entanglement. A divided panel of the Court of Appeals for the Fourth Circuit reversed. The majority relied primarily on the Lemon test but also took cognizance of Justice BREYER's *Van Orden* concurrence. While recognizing that the Commission acted for a secular purpose, the court held that the Bladensburg Cross failed *Lemon's* "effects" prong because a reasonable observer would view the Commission's ownership and maintenance of the monument as an endorsement of Christianity. . . .

[JUSTICE ALITO, joined by ROBERTS, C.J., and BREYER & KAVANAUGH, J.J., concluded that "the *Lemon* test presents particularly daunting problems in cases, including the one now before us, that involve the use, for ceremonial, celebratory, or commemorative purposes, of words or symbols with religious associations. . . *Lemon* ambitiously attempted to distill from the Court's existing case law a test that would bring order and predictability to Establishment Clause decisionmaking. That test, as noted, called on courts to examine the purposes and effects of a challenged government action, as well as any entanglement with religion that it might entail. . . If the *Lemon* Court thought that its test would provide a framework for all future Establishment Clause decisions, its expectation has not been met. In many cases, this Court has either expressly declined to apply the test or has simply ignored it. . . The test has been harshly criticized by Members of this Court, lamented by lower court judges, and questioned by a diverse roster of scholars. . . Together, these considerations counsel against efforts to evaluate such cases under *Lemon* and toward application of a presumption of constitutionality for longstanding monuments, symbols, and practices."]. . . .

These cases often concern monuments, symbols, or practices that were first established long ago, and in such cases, identifying their original purpose or purposes may be especially difficult. . . . The truth is that 70 years after the fact, there was no way to be certain about the motivations of the men who were responsible for the creation of the monument. And this is often the case with old monuments, symbols, and practices. Yet it would be inappropriate for courts to compel their removal or termination based on supposition. As time goes by, the purposes associated with an established monument, symbol, or practice often multiply. Take the example of Ten Commandments monuments, the subject we addressed in *Van Orden* and *McCreary County v. American Civil Liberties Union of Ky.* For believing Jews and Christians, the Ten Commandments are the word of God handed down to Moses on Mount Sinai, but the image of the Ten Commandments has also been used to convey other meanings. They have historical significance as one of the foundations of our legal system, and for largely that reason, they are depicted in the marble frieze in our courtroom and in other prominent public buildings in our Nation's capital. No Member of the Court thought that these depictions are unconstitutional. . . . Even if the original purpose of a monument was infused with religion, the passage of time may obscure that sentiment. . . .

Just as the purpose for maintaining a monument, symbol, or practice may evolve, "[t]he 'message' conveyed . . . may change over time." *Pleasant Grove City v. Summum.* Consider, for example, the message of the Statue of Liberty, which began as a monument to the solidarity and friendship between France and the United States and only decades later came to be seen as a beacon welcoming immigrants to a land of freedom. With sufficient time, religiously expressive monuments, symbols, and practices can become embedded features of a community's landscape and identity. In the same way, consider the many cities and towns across the United States that bear religious names. Religion undoubtedly motivated those who named Bethlehem, Pennsylvania; Las Cruces, New Mexico; Providence, Rhode Island; Corpus Christi, Texas; Nephi, Utah, and the countless other places in our country with names that are rooted in religion. Yet few would argue that this history requires that these names be erased from the map. . . . When time's passage imbues a religiously expressive monument, symbol, or practice with this kind of familiarity and historical significance, removing it may no longer appear neutral, especially to the local community for which it has taken on particular meaning. A government that roams the land, tearing down monuments with religious symbolism and scrubbing away any reference to the divine will strike many as aggressively hostile to religion. . . .

Retaining established, religiously expressive monuments, symbols, and practices is quite different from erecting or adopting new ones. The passage of time gives rise to a strong presumption of constitutionality. . . .

Applying these principles, we conclude that the Bladensburg Cross does not violate the Establishment Clause. That the cross originated as a Christian symbol and retains that meaning in many contexts does not change the fact that the symbol took on an added secular meaning when used in World War I memorials. . . . With the passage of time, it has acquired historical importance. It reminds the people of Bladensburg and surrounding areas of the deeds of their predecessors and of the sacrifices they made in a war fought in the name of democracy. The Cross now stands among memorials to veterans of later wars. It has become part of the community. . . .

Finally, it is surely relevant that the monument commemorates the death of particular individuals. It is natural and appropriate for those seeking to honor the deceased to invoke the symbols that signify what death meant for those who are memorialized. In some circumstances, the exclusion of any such recognition would make a memorial incomplete. This well explains why Holocaust memorials invariably include Stars of David or other symbols of Judaism. It explains why a new memorial to Native American veterans in Washington, D. C., will portray a steel circle to represent " 'the hole in the sky where the creator lives.' " And this is why the memorial for soldiers from the Bladensburg community features the cross—the same symbol that marks the graves of so many of their comrades near the battlefields where they fell.

The cross is undoubtedly a Christian symbol, but that fact should not blind us to everything else that the Bladensburg Cross has come to represent. For some, that monument is a symbolic resting place for ancestors who never returned home. For others, it is a place for the community to gather and honor all veterans and their sacrifices for our Nation. For others still, it is a historical landmark. For many of these people, destroying or defacing the Cross that has stood undisturbed for nearly a century would not be neutral and would not further the ideals of respect and tolerance embodied in the First Amendment. For all these reasons, the Cross does not offend the Constitution.

We reverse the judgment of the Court of Appeals for the Fourth Circuit and remand the cases for further proceedings.

It is so ordered.

JUSTICE BREYER, with whom JUSTICE KAGAN joins, concurring.

I have long maintained that there is no single formula for resolving Establishment Clause challenges. The Court must instead consider each case in light of the basic purposes that the Religion Clauses were meant to serve: assuring religious liberty and tolerance for all, avoiding religiously based social conflict, and maintaining that separation of church and state that allows each to flourish in its separate sphere. I agree with the Court that allowing the State of Maryland to display and maintain the Peace Cross poses no threat to those ends. And, as the Court explains, ordering its removal or alteration at this late date would signal "a hostility toward religion that has no place in our Establishment Clause traditions." Nor do I understand the Court's opinion today to adopt a "history and tradition test" that would permit any newly constructed religious memorial on public land. The Court appropriately "looks to history for guidance," but it upholds the constitutionality of the Peace Cross only after considering its particular historical context and its long-held place in the community. A newer memorial, erected under different circumstances, would not necessarily be permissible under this approach.

JUSTICE KAVANAUGH, concurring.

I have deep respect for the plaintiffs' sincere objections to seeing the cross on public land. I have great respect for the Jewish war veterans who in an amicus brief say that the cross on public land sends a message of exclusion. I recognize their sense of distress and alienation. Moreover, I fully understand the deeply religious nature of the cross. It would demean both believers and nonbelievers to say that the cross is not religious, or not all that religious. A case like this is difficult because it represents a clash of genuine and important interests. Applying our precedents, we uphold the constitutionality of the cross. In doing so, it is appropriate to also restate this bedrock constitutional principle: All citizens are equally American, no matter what religion they are, or if they have no religion at all.

JUSTICE GORSUCH, with whom JUSTICE THOMAS joins, concurring in the judgment.

The American Humanist Association wants a federal court to order the destruction of a 94 year-old war memorial because its members are offended. This "offended observer" theory of standing has no basis in law. Abandoning offended observer standing will mean only a return to the usual demands of Article III, requiring a real controversy with real impact on real persons to make a federal case out of it. Along the way, this will bring with it the welcome side effect of rescuing the federal judiciary from the sordid business of having to pass aesthetic judgment, one by one, on every public display in this country for its perceived capacity to give offense. It's a business that has consumed volumes of the federal reports, invited erratic results, frustrated generations of judges, and fomented the very kind of religiously based divisiveness that the Establishment Clause seeks to avoid.

JUSTICE GINSBURG, with whom JUSTICE SOTOMAYOR joins, dissenting.

. . .Decades ago, this Court recognized that the Establishment Clause of the First Amendment to the Constitution demands governmental neutrality among religious faiths, and between religion and nonreligion. Today the Court erodes that neutrality commitment, diminishing precedent designed to preserve individual liberty and civic harmony in favor of a "presumption of constitutionality for longstanding monuments, symbols, and practices."

The Latin cross is the foremost symbol of the Christian faith, embodying the central theological claim of Christianity: that the son of God died on the cross, that he rose from the dead, and that his death and resurrection offer the possibility of eternal life. . . . Using the cross as a war memorial does not transform it into a secular symbol, as the Courts of Appeals have uniformly recognized. By maintaining the Peace Cross on a public highway, the Commission elevates Christianity over other faiths, and religion over nonreligion. . . .

In cases challenging the government's display of a religious symbol, the Court has tested fidelity to the principle of neutrality by asking whether the display has the "effect of 'endorsing' religion." *County of Allegheny v. American Civil Liberties Union, Greater Pittsburgh Chapter.* As I see it, when a cross is displayed on public property, the government may be presumed to endorse its religious content. The venue is surely associated with the State; the symbol and its meaning are just as surely associated exclusively with Christianity. . . . A presumption of endorsement, of course, may be overcome. The "typical museum setting," for example, "though not neutralizing the religious content of a religious painting, negates any message of endorsement of that content." *Lynch v. Donnelly.* Similarly, when a public school history teacher discusses the Protestant Reformation, the setting makes clear that the teacher's purpose is to educate, not to proselytize. The Peace Cross, however, is not of that genre.

For nearly two millennia, the Latin cross has been the defining symbol of Christianity, evoking the foundational claims of that faith. Christianity teaches that Jesus Christ was "a divine Savior" who "illuminate[d] a path toward salvation and redemption." *Lynch.* Central to the religion are the beliefs that "the son of God," Jesus Christ, "died on the cross," that "he rose from the dead," and that "his death and resurrection offer the possibility of eternal life." Brief for *Amici* Christian and Jewish Organizations. An exclusively Christian symbol, the Latin cross is not emblematic of any other faith.

The Commission urges in defense of its monument that the Latin cross "is not merely a reaffirmation of Christian beliefs"; rather, "when used in the context of a war memorial," the cross becomes "a universal symbol of the sacrifices of those who fought and died." The Commission's "[a]ttempts to secularize what is unquestionably a sacred [symbol] defy credibility and disserve people of faith." *Van Orden* (Stevens, J. dissenting). The asserted commemorative meaning of the cross rests on— and is inseparable from—its Christian meaning: "the crucifixion of Jesus Christ and the redeeming benefits of his passion and death," specifically, "the salvation of man." Every Court of Appeals to confront the question has held that "[m]aking a . . . Latin cross a war memorial does not make the cross secular," it "makes the war memorial sectarian." *Salazar v. Buono,* 559 U.S. at 747. . . .

The Commission nonetheless urges that the Latin cross is a "well-established" secular symbol commemorating, in particular, "military valor and sacrifice [in] World War I." The Commission overlooks this reality: The cross was never perceived as an appropriate headstone or memorial for Jewish soldiers and others who did not adhere to Christianity. . . .

When the War Department began preparing designs for permanent headstones in 1919, no topic managed to stir more controversy than the use of religious symbolism. Everyone involved in the dispute, however, saw the Latin cross as a Christian symbol, not as a universal or secular one. . . . Throughout the headstone debate, no one doubted that the Latin cross and the Star of David were sectarian gravemarkers, and therefore appropriate only for soldiers who adhered to those faiths. The Court lists just seven freestanding cross memorials, less than 1% of the total number of monuments to World War I in the United States. Cross memorials are outliers. The overwhelming majority of World War I memorials contain no Latin cross. In fact, the most popular and enduring memorial of the post-World War I decade was the mass-produced *Spirit of the American Doughboy* statue. . . .

Holding the Commission's display of the Peace Cross unconstitutional would not, as the Commission fears, "inevitably require the destruction of other cross-shaped memorials throughout the country." Like the determination of the violation itself, the proper remedy is necessarily context specific. In some instances, the violation may be cured by relocating the monument to private land or by transferring ownership of the land and monument to a private party. . . .

The Establishment Clause, which preserves the integrity of both church and state, guarantees that "however . . . individuals worship, they will count as full and equal American citizens." *Town of Greece,* 572 U.S. at 615 (KAGAN, J., dissenting). "If the aim of the Establishment Clause is genuinely to uncouple government from church," the Clause does "not permit . . . a display of th[e] character" of Bladensburg's Peace Cross.

Capitol Square Review and Advisory Bd. v. Pinette, 515 U.S. 753 (GINSBURG, J., dissenting).

The Bladensburg Peace Cross. App. 887.

[The concurring opinions of KAGAN, J., and THOMAS, J. are omitted.]

11–3   RELIGIOUSLY BASED EXCEPTIONS TO STATE IMPOSED DUTIES

Unabridged, p. 1447; add to Note 3, after *Cutter v. Wilkinson*:

Abridged, p. 1109; add to end of Note 2:

Holt v. Hobbs, 574 U.S. ___, 135 S.Ct. 853, 190 L.Ed.2d 747 (2015). A Muslim prisoner wanted to grow a ½-inch beard in accordance with his religious beliefs. He sued the Director of Arkansas Department of Correction, challenging under the Religious Land Use and Institutionalized Persons Act (RLUIPA) the denial of a religious accommodation under Department's grooming policy. Alito, J., for the Court, held that this grooming policy substantially burdened the prisoner's exercise of religion. The Department does have a compelling interest in preventing prisoners from hiding contraband, or disguising their identities, but this beard policy is not the least restrictive means of implementing that interest. The prison could not show why the security risk presented by a prisoner shaving a ½-inch beard is so different from the risk of a prisoner shaving a mustache, head hair, or ¼-inch beard. Similarly, the prison did not explain why the risk that a prisoner will shave a ½-inch beard to disguise himself is so great that the prison cannot allow ½-inch beards even though it allows prisoners to grow mustaches, head hair, or ¼-inch beards for medical/ dermatological reasons.

The district court was also erred in suggesting that the burden on the prisoner's religious exercise was slight because he testified that his religion would "credit" him for attempting to follow his religious beliefs, even if that attempt proved to be unsuccessful. "RLUIPA, however, applies to an exercise of religion regardless of whether it is 'compelled.' "

Unabridged, p. 1450; add to end of Note 4:

Abridged, p. 1110; add to end of Note 3:

   Zubik v. Burwell, 578 U.S. ___, 136 S.Ct. 1557, 194 L.Ed.2d 269 (2016)(per curiam). Various nonprofit religious groups, led by the Little Sisters of the Poor (an order of Catholic nuns who run hospices), objected that the Secretary of Health and Human Services required them to offer an insurance plan including abortion-causing drugs. They had no problem with the federal government providing such services or the Government paying for them. They just did not want to be complicit.

   During the oral argument, Justice Alito asked the Solicitor General whether it was a substantial burden for a female employee of a religious organization to go on her state exchange to purchase a separate contraceptive policy (which the federal government could pay for if it wanted to do so). The Solicitor General responded that it was a "hassle" to use the state or federal exchange, but Chief Justice Roberts (perhaps smiling) said, "I've heard about how easy it is [to use the health exchanges]." The Government argued that its mandate was necessary for employees to have "seamless coverage, but Petitioners argued that the Government tolerated or created non-seamless coverage for millions of other employees.[1]

   The petitioners' briefs pointed out that "tens of millions of people" are in grandfathered plans not subject to the mandate, and there is no requirement that these plans "ever be phased out." The Government's purpose for exempting millions from this contraception/abortifacients mandate is merely to "promote administrative convenience."[2] The Government also exempts millions of other employees from this contraceptive/abortifacients coverage because they work for small employers, or, Petitioners argued, the Government created arcane or irrational distinctions.[3] Petitioners argued that this Government mandate is not a neutral law of general applicability that governed religious and nonreligious alike.

---

   [1] Petitioners argued, because "the Government has decided not to mandate contraceptive coverage at all in connection with grandfathered plans and [certain] 'religious employer' plans, it cannot claim a compelling interest in mandating 'seamless' coverage in connection with Petitioners' plans." Brief of Petitioners, *Zubik v. Burwell*, 2016 WL 93988 *70 (U.S. 2016).

   [2] The Government estimated that 37% of private employers in the country offer at least one grandfathered health plan, and 26% of employees nationwide are enrolled in a grandfathered plan. "In total, at least 33.9 million people are on private-sector grandfathered plans, and 10.7 million people are on state- and local-government grandfathered plans. See 80 Fed. Reg. 72,192, 72,218 (Nov. 18, 2015)." Brief of Petitioners, *Zubik v. Burwell*, 2016 WL 93988 * 7 (U.S. 2016).

   [3] For example, the Government did not exempt the Catholic Charities of Pittsburgh because it is incorporated separately from the Diocese of Pittsburgh. Its counterpart, Catholic Charities of Erie, is a department of the Roman Catholic Diocese of Erie. Because of this formal difference, the Government ordered Catholic Charities of Pittsburgh to comply with the mandate but not the Catholic Charities of Erie which was considered part of an "exempt" religious employer. Brief of Petitioners, *Zubik v. Burwell*, 2016 WL 93988 *58 (U.S. 2016).

After oral argument, the Court took the unusual step of asking the litigants to submit supplemental briefs on whether there could be an "accommodation" to avoid compromising religious convictions. The religious groups proposed that the federal government require insurance companies to create stand-alone contraception plans for workers at religiously affiliated institutions "with separate enrollment processes, insurance cards, payment sources, and communication streams." The petitioners' brief explained, "Under a truly independent scheme, such employers wouldn't be complying with that mandate at all. They would be exempt from that mandate, and the commercial insurer would be complying with a separate mandate imposed by the federal government." The Government "confirmed that the challenged procedures 'for employers with insured plans could be modified to operate in the manner posited in the Court's order while still ensuring that the affected women receive contraceptive coverage seamlessly, together with the rest of their health coverage.' " Consequently, the Court remanded to give the parties the opportunity to "arrive at an approach going forward that accommodates petitioners' religious exercise while at the same time ensuring that women covered by petitioners' health plans "receive full and equal health coverage, including contraceptive coverage."

In the meantime, "the Government may not impose taxes or penalties on petitioners for failure to provide the relevant notice." The Court added that it expressed no view on the merits of the case. Sotomayor, J., concurred, joined by Ginsburg, J., noting that the lower courts should not construe today's opinion as an expression of the Court's views on the merits.

Unabridged, p. 1450; add to end of *Notes*, new Note 5:

Abridged, p. 1110; add to end of *Notes*, new Note 4:

Masterpiece Cakeshop, Ltd. v. Colorado Civil Rights Commission, 138 S.Ct. 1719 (2018). Masterpiece Cakeshop is a Colorado bakery owned and operated by Jack Phillips. In 2012 a same-sex couple visited Phillip's bakery to order a cake for their wedding reception. Phillips, a devout Christian who opposes same-sex marriage, refused to create a cake for their wedding. Colorado at the time did not recognize the legality of same-sex marriages. The couple filed a complaint with the Colorado Civil Rights Commission alleging discrimination based on sexual orientation in violation of Colorado's Anti-Discrimination Act. The Commission determined that the shop's actions violated the Act and the Colorado state courts affirmed. Kennedy, J., for the Court (7–2), reversed. The Court noted the "difficult questions" of reconciling the rights and dignity of gay persons who wish to be married but who face discrimination when they seek goods or services with the right of all persons to exercise fundamental freedoms under the First Amendment. The Court did not resolve this "difficult question." The Court instead found that the Colorado Civil Rights Commission's consideration of this case "was inconsistent with the State's obligation of religious neutrality." The Commission did not give Phillips the "neutral and respectful consideration" to which he was entitled. During the public hearing on the matter some commissioners endorsed the view that religious beliefs cannot legitimately be carried into the public sphere or commercial domain; that Phillips invocation of sincerely held religious beliefs were comparable to defenses of slavery and the Holocaust; and described Phillip's faith as "one of the most despicable pieces of rhetoric that people can use." No objection was made to these remarks. "The Court cannot avoid the conclusion that these statements cast doubt on the fairness and impartiality of the Commission's adjudication of Phillip's case." *Church of Lukumi Babalu Aye, Inc. v. Hialeah,* 508 U.S. 520, 540–542 (1993). Thomas, J., joined by Gorsuch, J. concurred, arguing that Phillips was denied not only his right to freely exercise his religion but also his right to free speech. Phillips, they noted, is an artistic baker, and his creation and designing custom wedding cakes is expressive conduct. As such, Colorado's public accommodations law cannot penalize it unless it withstands strict scrutiny.

In *Trump v. Hawaii* [supra, p. 37], the Court did not deny that the President's statements discriminated on the basis of religion and appeared not to give "neutral and respectful consideration" of Islam. However, in contrast to *Masterpiece Cakeshop,* the Court, citing *Kleindienst v. Mandel,* did not look behind the President's Executive Order to determine whether it was motivated by religious animus. According to Justice Sotomayor, the correct test to decide Establishment Clause claims is "whether a reasonable observer would view the government's action as enacted for the purpose of disfavoring a religion." Does the Court use a different standard for reviewing domestic claims involving Establishment Clause violations, such as religious displays and school prayer, and cases involving foreign affairs such as national security directives regulating the entry of aliens abroad? The answer appears to be that different tests are used. Is there a principled basis for that distinction?

Unabridged, p. 1450; add new case after the *Notes*:

Abridged, p. 1110; add new case after the *Notes*:

TRINITY LUTHERAN CHURCH OF COLUMBIA, INC. V. COMER
137 S.Ct. 2012, 198 L.Ed.2d 551 (2017).

CHIEF JUSTICE ROBERTS delivered the opinion of the Court, except as to footnote 3.

The Missouri Department of Natural Resources offers state grants to help public and private schools, nonprofit daycare centers, and other nonprofit entities purchase rubber playground surfaces made from recycled tires. Trinity Lutheran Church applied for such a grant for its preschool and daycare center and would have received one, but for the fact that Trinity Lutheran is a church. The Department had a policy of categorically disqualifying churches and other religious organizations from receiving grants under its playground resurfacing program. The question presented is whether the Department's policy violated the rights of Trinity Lutheran under the Free Exercise Clause of the First Amendment.

The Trinity Lutheran Church Child Learning Center is a preschool and daycare center open throughout the year to serve working families in Boone County, Missouri, and the surrounding area. [T]he Center merged with Trinity Lutheran Church in 1985 and operates under its auspices on church property. The Center admits students of any religion, and enrollment stands at about 90 children ranging from age two to five.

The Center includes a playground that is equipped with the basic playground essentials: slides, swings, jungle gyms, monkey bars, and sandboxes. Almost the entire surface beneath and surrounding the play equipment is coarse pea gravel. Youngsters, of course, often fall on the playground or tumble from the equipment. And when they do, the gravel can be unforgiving.

In 2012, the Center sought to replace a large portion of the pea gravel with a pour-in-place rubber surface by participating in Missouri's Scrap Tire Program. Run by the State's Department of Natural Resources to reduce the number of used tires destined for landfills and dump sites, the program offers reimbursement grants to qualifying nonprofit organizations that purchase playground surfaces made from recycled tires. It is funded through a fee imposed on the sale of new tires in the State.

Due to limited resources, the Department cannot offer grants to all applicants and so awards them on a competitive basis to those scoring highest based on several criteria, such as the poverty level of the population in the surrounding area and the applicant's plan to promote recycling. When the Center applied, the Department had a strict and express policy of denying grants to any applicant owned or controlled by a church, sect, or other religious entity. That policy, in the Department's view, was compelled by Article I, Section 7 of the Missouri Constitution, which provides:

> "That no money shall ever be taken from the public treasury, directly or indirectly, in aid of any church, sect or denomination of religion, or in aid of any priest, preacher, minister or teacher thereof, as such; and that no preference shall be given to nor any discrimination made against any church, sect or creed of religion, or any form of religious faith or worship."

In its application, the Center disclosed its status as a ministry of Trinity Lutheran Church and specified that the Center's mission was "to provide a safe, clean, and attractive school facility in conjunction with an educational program structured to allow a child to grow spiritually, physically, socially, and cognitively." App. to Pet. for Cert. 131a. . . .

The Center ranked fifth among the 44 applicants in the 2012 Scrap Tire Program. But despite its high score, the Center was deemed categorically ineligible to receive a grant. [T]he program director explained that, under Article I, Section 7 of the Missouri Constitution, the Department could not provide financial assistance directly to a church. The Department ultimately awarded 14 grants as part of the 2012 program. Because the Center was operated by Trinity Lutheran Church, it did not receive a grant.

Trinity Lutheran sued the Director of the Department in Federal District Court. The Church alleged that the Department's failure to approve the Center's application, pursuant to its policy of denying grants to religiously affiliated applicants, violates the Free Exercise Clause of the First Amendment. Trinity Lutheran sought declaratory and injunctive relief prohibiting the Department from discriminating against the Church on that basis in future grant applications.

The District Court granted the Department's motion to dismiss [and] the Eighth Circuit affirmed. The court recognized that it was "rather clear" that Missouri *could* award a scrap tire grant to Trinity Lutheran without running afoul of the Establishment Clause of the United States Constitution. But, the Court of Appeals explained, that did not mean the Free Exercise Clause compelled the State to disregard the antiestablishment principle reflected in its own Constitution. . . . We granted certiorari and now reverse.

The First Amendment provides, in part, that "Congress shall make no law respecting an establishment of religion, or prohibiting the free exercise thereof." The parties agree that the Establishment Clause of that Amendment does not prevent Missouri from including Trinity Lutheran in the Scrap Tire Program. That does not, however, answer the question under the Free Exercise Clause, because we have recognized that there is "play in the joints" between what the Establishment Clause permits and the Free Exercise Clause compels. *Locke* [*v. Davey*] (internal quotation marks omitted).*

The Free Exercise Clause "protect[s] religious observers against unequal treatment" and subjects to the strictest scrutiny laws that target the religious for "special disabilities" based on their "religious status." *Church of Lukumi Babalu Aye, Inc. v. Hialeah*, 508 U.S. 520, 533, 542 (1993) (internal quotation marks omitted). Applying that basic principle, this Court has repeatedly confirmed that denying a generally available

---

* [Editor's Note: *Locke v. Davey*, 540 U.S. 712, 124 S.Ct. 1307, 158 L.Ed.2d 1 (2004), held that a state did not violate Free Exercise Clause by refusing to fund devotional theology instruction.]

benefit solely on account of religious identity imposes a penalty on the free exercise of religion that can be justified only by a state interest 'of the highest order.' *McDaniel v. Paty*, 435 U.S. 618, 628 (1978) (plurality opinion) (quoting *Wisconsin v. Yoder*, 406 U.S. 205, 215 (1972)).

In *Everson v. Board of Education of Ewing*, 330 U.S. 1 (1947), for example, we upheld against an Establishment Clause challenge a New Jersey law enabling a local school *district* to reimburse parents for the public transportation costs of sending their children to public and private schools, including parochial schools. In the course of ruling that the Establishment Clause allowed New Jersey to extend that public benefit to all its citizens regardless of their religious belief, we explained that a State 'cannot hamper its citizens in the free exercise of their own religion. Consequently, it cannot exclude individual Catholics, Lutherans, Mohammedans, Baptists, Jews, Methodists, Non-believers, Presbyterians, or the members of any other faith, *because of their faith, or lack of it*, from receiving the benefits of public welfare legislation.' *Id.*, at 16.

Three decades later, in *McDaniel v. Paty*, the Court struck down under the Free Exercise Clause a Tennessee statute disqualifying ministers from serving as delegates to the State's constitutional convention. Writing for the plurality, Chief Justice Burger acknowledged that Tennessee had disqualified ministers from serving as legislators since the adoption of its first Constitution in 1796, and that a number of early States had also disqualified ministers from legislative office. This historical tradition, however, did not change the fact that the statute discriminated against McDaniel by denying him a benefit solely because of his "*status* as a 'minister.'" McDaniel could not seek to participate in the convention while also maintaining his role as a minister; to pursue the one, he would have to give up the other. In this way, said Chief Justice Burger, the Tennessee law "effectively penalizes the free exercise of [McDaniel's] constitutional liberties," quoting *Sherbert v. Verner*, (1963); internal quotation marks omitted). Joined by Justice Marshall in concurrence, Justice Brennan added that "because the challenged provision requires [McDaniel] to purchase his right to engage in the ministry by sacrificing his candidacy it impairs the free exercise of his religion." *McDaniel*, 435 U.S., at 634.

In recent years, when this Court has rejected free exercise challenges, the laws in question have been neutral and generally applicable without regard to religion. We have been careful to distinguish such laws from those that single out the religious for disfavored treatment.

For example, in *Lyng v. Northwest Indian Cemetery Protective Association*, 485 U.S. 439 (1988), we held that the Free Exercise Clause did not prohibit the Government from timber harvesting or road construction on a particular tract of federal land, even though the Government's action would obstruct the religious practice of several Native American Tribes that held certain sites on the tract to be sacred. . . . The Court specifically noted, however, that the Government action did not "penalize religious activity by denying any person an equal share of the rights, benefits, and privileges enjoyed by other citizens."

[I]n *Church of Lukumi Babalu Aye, Inc. v. Hialeah*, we struck down three facially neutral city ordinances that outlawed certain forms of animal slaughter. Members of the Santeria religion challenged the ordinances under the Free Exercise Clause, alleging that despite their facial neutrality, the ordinances had a discriminatory purpose easy to ferret out: prohibiting sacrificial rituals integral to Santeria but distasteful to local residents. We agreed. [C]iting *McDaniel* and *Smith*, we restated the now-familiar refrain: The Free Exercise Clause protects against laws that " 'impose[ ] special disabilities on the basis of . . . religious status.' "

The Department's policy expressly discriminates against otherwise eligible recipients by disqualifying them from a public benefit solely because of their religious character. If the cases just described make one thing clear, it is that such a policy imposes a penalty on the free exercise of religion that triggers the most exacting scrutiny. This conclusion is unremarkable in light of our prior decisions.

Like the disqualification statute in *McDaniel*, the Department's policy puts Trinity Lutheran to a choice: It may participate in an otherwise available benefit program or remain a religious institution. Of course, Trinity Lutheran is free to continue operating as a church, just as McDaniel was free to continue being a minister. But that freedom comes at the cost of automatic and absolute exclusion from the benefits of a public program for which the Center is otherwise fully qualified. And when the State conditions a benefit in this way, *McDaniel* says plainly that the State has punished the free exercise of religion: "To condition the availability of benefits . . . upon [a recipient's] willingness to . . . surrender[ ] his religiously impelled [status] effectively penalizes the free exercise of his constitutional liberties." (plurality opinion) (alterations omitted).

The Department contends that merely declining to extend funds to Trinity Lutheran does not *prohibit* the Church from engaging in any religious conduct or otherwise exercising its religious rights. In this sense, says the Department, its policy is unlike the ordinances struck down in *Lukumi*, which outlawed rituals central to Santeria. Here the Department has simply declined to allocate to Trinity Lutheran a subsidy the State had no obligation to provide in the first place. That decision does not meaningfully burden the Church's free exercise rights. And absent any such burden, the argument continues, the Department is free to heed the State's antiestablishment objection to providing funds directly to a church.

It is true the Department has not criminalized the way Trinity Lutheran worships or told the Church that it cannot subscribe to a certain view of the Gospel. But, as the Department itself acknowledges, the Free Exercise Clause protects against "indirect coercion or penalties on the free exercise of religion, not just outright prohibitions." *Lyng.* As the Court put it more than 50 years ago, "[i]t is too late in the day to doubt that the liberties of religion and expression may be infringed by the denial of or placing of conditions upon a benefit or privilege." *Sherbert*; see also *McDaniel*, 435 U.S., at 633 (Brennan, J., concurring in judgment) (The 'proposition—that the law does not interfere with free exercise because it does not directly prohibit religious activity, but merely conditions eligibility for office on its abandonment—is . . . squarely rejected by precedent').

Trinity Lutheran is not claiming any entitlement to a subsidy. It instead asserts a right to participate in a government benefit program without having to disavow its religious character. The "imposition of such a condition upon even a gratuitous benefit inevitably deter[s] or discourage[s] the exercise of First Amendment rights." The express discrimination against religious exercise here is not the denial of a grant, but rather the refusal to allow the Church—solely because it is a church—to compete with secular organizations for a grant.

The Department attempts to get out from under the weight of our precedents by arguing that the free exercise question in this case is instead controlled by our decision in *Locke v. Davey.* It is not. In *Locke*, the State of Washington created a scholarship program to assist high-achieving students with the costs of postsecondary education. The scholarships were paid out of the State's general fund, and eligibility was based on criteria such as an applicant's score on college admission tests and family income. While scholarship recipients were free to use the money at accredited religious and non-religious schools alike, they were not permitted to use the funds to pursue a devotional theology degree—one "devotional in nature or designed to induce religious faith." (internal quotation marks omitted). Davey was selected for a scholarship but was denied the funds when he refused to certify that he would not use them toward a devotional degree. He sued, arguing that the State's refusal to allow its scholarship money to go toward such degrees violated his free exercise rights.

This Court disagreed. [T]he State had "merely chosen not to fund a distinct category of instruction." Davey was not denied a scholarship because of who he *was*; he was denied a scholarship because of what he proposed *to do*—use the funds to prepare for the ministry. Here there is no question that Trinity Lutheran was denied a grant simply because of what it is—a church.

The Court in *Locke* also stated that Washington's choice was in keeping with the State's antiestablishment interest in not using taxpayer funds to pay for the training of clergy; in fact, the Court could "think of few areas in which a State's antiestablishment interests come more into play." The claimant in *Locke* sought funding for an "essentially religious endeavor . . . akin to a religious calling as well as an academic pursuit," and opposition to such funding "to support church leaders" lay at the historic core of the Religion Clauses. Here nothing of the sort can be said about a program to use recycled tires to resurface playgrounds.

. . . *Locke* took account of Washington's antiestablishment interest only after determining, as noted, that the scholarship program did not "require students to choose between their religious beliefs and receiving a government benefit." 540 U.S., at 720–721 (citing *McDaniel*, 435 U.S. 618). As the Court put it, Washington's scholarship program went "a long way toward including religion in its benefits." Students in the program were free to use their scholarships at "pervasively religious schools." Davey could use his scholarship to pursue a secular degree at one institution while studying devotional theology at another. He could also use his scholarship money to attend a religious college and take devotional theology courses there. The only thing he could not do was use the scholarship to pursue a degree in that subject.

In this case, there is no dispute that Trinity Lutheran *is* put to the choice between being a church and receiving a government benefit. The rule is simple: No churches need apply.[3]

The State in this case expressly requires Trinity Lutheran to renounce its religious character in order to participate in an otherwise generally available public benefit program, for which it is fully qualified. Our cases make clear that such a condition imposes a penalty on the free exercise of religion that must be subjected to the "most rigorous" scrutiny. *Lukumi*.[4] . . .

The State has pursued its preferred policy to the point of expressly denying a qualified religious entity a public benefit solely because of its

---

[3]   This case involves express discrimination based on religious identity with respect to playground resurfacing. We do not address religious uses of funding or other forms of discrimination.

[4]   We have held that "a law targeting religious beliefs as such is never permissible." *Lukumi*; see also *McDaniel v. Paty* (1978) (plurality opinion). We do not need to decide whether the condition Missouri imposes in this case falls within the scope of that rule, because it cannot survive strict scrutiny in any event.

religious character. Under our precedents, that goes too far. The Department's policy violates the Free Exercise Clause. . . .

JUSTICE GORSUCH, with whom JUSTICE THOMAS joins, concurring in part.

Missouri's law bars Trinity Lutheran from participating in a public benefits program only because it is a church. I agree this violates the First Amendment and I am pleased to join nearly all of the Court's opinion. I offer only two modest qualifications.

First, the Court leaves open the possibility a useful distinction might be drawn between laws that discriminate on the basis of religious *status* and religious *use*. Respectfully, I harbor doubts about the stability of such a line. Does a religious man say grace before dinner? Or does a man begin his meal in a religious manner? Is it a religious group that built the playground? Or did a group build the playground so it might be used to advance a religious mission? . . .

Neither do I see why the First Amendment's Free Exercise Clause should care. After all, that Clause guarantees the free *exercise* of religion, not just the right to inward belief (or status). And this Court has long explained that government may not "devise mechanisms, overt or disguised, designed to persecute or oppress a religion or its practices." Generally, the government may not force people to choose between participation in a public program and their right to free exercise of religion. I don't see why it should matter whether we describe that benefit, say, as closed to Lutherans (status) or closed to people who do Lutheran things (use). It is free exercise either way.

For these reasons, reliance on the status-use distinction does not suffice for me to distinguish *Locke v. Davey*, 540 U.S. 712 (2004). In that case, this Court upheld a funding restriction barring a student from using a scholarship to pursue a degree in devotional theology. But can it really matter whether the restriction in *Locke* was phrased in terms of use instead of status (for was it a student who wanted a vocational degree in religion? or was it a religious student who wanted the necessary education for his chosen vocation?). If that case can be correct and distinguished, it seems it might be only because of the opinion's claim of a long tradition against the use of public funds for training of the clergy, a tradition the Court correctly explains has no analogue here.

Second and for similar reasons, I am unable to join the footnoted observation, n. 3, that "[t]his case involves express discrimination based on religious identity with respect to playground resurfacing." Of course the footnote is entirely correct, but I worry that some might mistakenly read it to suggest that only "playground resurfacing" cases, or only those with some association with children's safety or health, or perhaps some other social good we find sufficiently worthy, are governed by the legal rules recounted in and faithfully applied by the Court's opinion. Such a reading would be unreasonable for our cases are "governed by general principles, rather than ad hoc improvisations." And the general principles here do not permit discrimination against religious exercise—whether on the playground or anywhere else.

JUSTICE BREYER, concurring in the judgment. . . .

The Court stated in *Everson* that "cutting off church schools from" such "general government services as ordinary police and fire protection . . . is obviously not the purpose of the First Amendment." Here, the State would cut Trinity Lutheran off from participation in a general program designed to secure or to improve the health and safety of children. I see no significant difference. The fact that the program at issue ultimately funds only a limited number of projects cannot itself justify a religious distinction. Nor is there any administrative or other reason to treat church schools differently. The sole reason advanced that explains the difference is faith. And it is that last-mentioned fact that calls the Free Exercise Clause into play. We need not go further. Public benefits come in many shapes and sizes. I would leave the application of the Free Exercise Clause to other kinds of public benefits for another day.

JUSTICE SOTOMAYOR, with whom JUSTICE GINSBURG joins, dissenting.

To hear the Court tell it, this is a simple case about recycling tires to resurface a playground. The stakes are higher. This case is about nothing less than the relationship between religious institutions and the civil government—that is, between church and state. The Court today profoundly changes that relationship by holding, for the first time, that the Constitution requires the government to provide public funds directly to a church. Its decision slights both our precedents and our history, and its reasoning weakens this country's longstanding commitment to a separation of church and state beneficial to both.

Founded in 1922, Trinity Lutheran Church (Church) "operates . . . for the express purpose of carrying out the commission of . . . Jesus Christ as directed to His church on earth" Our Story, http://www.trinity-lcms.org/story (all internet materials as last visited June 22, 2017). The Church uses "preaching, teaching, worship, witness, service, and fellowship according to the Word of God" to carry out its mission "to 'make disciples.'" Mission, http://www.trinity-lcms.org/mission (quoting Matthew 28:18–20). The Church's religious beliefs include its desire to "associat[e] with the [Trinity Church Child] Learning Center." App. to Pet. for Cert. Located on Church property, the Learning Center provides daycare and preschool for about "90 children ages two to kindergarten." *Id.*

The Learning Center serves as "a ministry of the Church and incorporates daily religion and developmentally appropriate activities into . . . [its] program." *Id.* In this way, "[t]hrough the Learning Center, the Church teaches a Christian world view to children of members of the Church, as well as children of non-member residents" of the area. These activities represent the Church's "sincere religious belief . . . to use [the Learning Center] to teach the Gospel to children of its members, as well to bring the Gospel message to non-members."

[I]t is surprising that the Court mentions the Establishment Clause only to note the parties' agreement that it "does not prevent Missouri from including Trinity Lutheran in the Scrap Tire Program." Constitutional questions are decided by this Court, not the parties' concessions. The Establishment Clause does not allow Missouri to grant the Church's funding request because the Church uses the Learning Center, including its playground, in conjunction with its religious mission. The Court's silence on this front signals either its misunderstanding of the facts of this case or a startling departure from our precedents.

. . . The Church seeks state funds to improve the Learning Center's facilities, which, by the Church's own avowed description, are used to assist the spiritual growth of the children of its members and to spread the Church's faith to the children of nonmembers. The Church's playground surface—like a Sunday School room's walls or the sanctuary's pews—are integrated with and integral to its religious mission. The conclusion that the funding the Church seeks would impermissibly advance religion is inescapable.

[A] prophylactic rule against the use of public funds for houses of worship is a permissible accommodation of these weighty interests. . . . Today, thirty-eight States have a counterpart to Missouri's Article I, § 7. The provisions, as a general matter, date back to or before these States' original Constitutions. That so many States have for so long drawn a line that prohibits public funding for houses of worship, based on principles rooted in this Nation's understanding of how best to foster religious liberty, supports the conclusion that public funding of houses of worship "is of a different ilk."

. . . The Scrap Tire Program offers not a generally available benefit but a selective benefit for a few recipients each year. In this context, the comparison to truly generally available benefits is inapt.

On top of all of this, the Court's application of its new rule here is mistaken. . . . The constitutional provisions of thirty-nine States—all but invalidated today—the weighty interests they protect, and the history they draw on deserve more than this judicial brush aside. . . .

Today's decision discounts centuries of history and jeopardizes the government's ability to remain secular. . . .

The Court today dismantles a core protection for religious freedom provided in these Clauses. It holds not just that a government may support houses of worship with taxpayer funds, but that—at least in this case and perhaps in others,—it must do so whenever it decides to create a funding program. History shows that the Religion Clauses separate the public treasury from religious coffers as one measure to secure the kind of freedom of conscience that benefits both religion and government. If this separation means anything, it means that the government cannot, or at the very least need not, tax its citizens and turn that money over to houses of worship. The Court today blinds itself to the outcome this history requires and leads us instead to a place where separation of church and state is a constitutional slogan, not a constitutional commitment. I dissent.

[The Opinion of THOMAS, J., joined by GORSUCH, J., concurring in part, is omitted.]

NOTES

1. The dissent notes that Missouri's Constitutional provision in this case is found in thirty-nine States and they are "all but invalidated today." These amendments are often called Blaine Amendments, which historians say were rooted in 19th century anti-Catholic bigotry. They were designed to prevent any state aid that might go to Catholic parochial schools.* Republican Congressman (and then Senator) James G. Blaine from Maine proposed a federal constitutional amendment to forbid any use of public funds to support religious schools, which were typically Catholic. That proposed U.S. Constitutional Amendment did not pass Congress, but many states enacted versions of the Blaine Amendment and some states have used them to deny school aid or vouchers to religiously affiliated schools.

Note that in footnote 4 the Court says, "We have held that 'a law targeting religious beliefs as such is never permissible.' We do not need to decide whether the condition Missouri imposes in this case falls within the scope of that rule, because it cannot survive strict scrutiny in any event." (Internal citations omitted). Hence, the Court did not examine whether the state versions of the Blaine Amendment were unconstitutional as intending to target a particular religion.

---

* See, *e.g.,* U.S. Commission on Civil Rights, *School Choice: The Blaine Amendments & Anti-Catholicism* (2007), http://www.usccr.gov/pubs/BlaineReport.pdf; PHILIP HAMBURGER, SEPARATION OF CHURCH AND STATE 335 (Harvard Univ. Press, 2002) (Nativist Protestants "failed to obtain a federal constitutional amendment but, because of the strength of anti-Catholic feeling, managed to secure local versions of the Blaine amendment in the vast majority of the states.") Douglas Laycock, *The Underlying Unity of Separation and Neutrality*, 46 Emory L.J. 43, 50 (1997)("Although there were legitimate arguments made on both sides, the nineteenth century opposition to funding religious schools drew heavily on anti-Catholicism. Nativist opposition to Catholic immigration fluctuated after 1825, but it never disappeared.")

2. The day after the Court decided *Trinity Lutheran*, it vacated and remanded two cases in light of *Trinity Lutheran*: (1) a New Mexico Supreme Court decision that prevented students at religious schools from receiving state-funded textbooks, *New Mexico Ass'n of Non-public Schools v. Moses*, 137 S.Ct. 2325 (2017), and (2), a Colorado Supreme Court ruling that prohibited a school choice program, because students at religious schools were allowed to participate. *Colorado State Board of Education v. Taxpayers for Public Education*, 137 S.Ct. 2325 (2017).

CHAPTER 12

THE PROCEDURAL CONTEXT OF CONSTITUTIONAL LITIGATION

■ ■ ■

12–4 NONTAXPAYER STANDING

12–4.1 THE REQUIREMENT OF "INJURY IN FACT" AND "CAUSAL CONNECTION"

Unabridged, p. 1493; add to end of *Notes*, new Note 5:

5. *Department of Commerce et al. v. New York, et al.,* 139 S.Ct. 2551 (2019). Two groups of plaintiffs challenged in federal court the decision by the Secretary of Commerce to reinstate a question about citizenship on the 2020 census questionnaire. The first group of plaintiffs included 18 states, the District of Columbia, various counties and cities, and the United States Conference of Mayors. The second group of plaintiffs consisted of several non-governmental organizations that work with immigrant and minority communities. The plaintiffs asserted several types of injuries based on their expectation that reinstating a citizenship question would depress the census response rate and lead to an inaccurate population count. The expected injuries included diminishment of political representation, loss of federal funds, degradation of census date, and diversion of resources. Several states with a disproportionate share of noncitizens, for example, anticipate losing a seat in Congress or qualifying for less federal funding if their populations are undercounted. The Court, in an opinion by Roberts, C.J., agreed that at least some plaintiffs have Article III standing. Several states have shown that if noncitizen households are undercounted by as little as 2%, they will lose federal funds. "That is a sufficiently concrete and imminent injury to satisfy Article III." And a ruling in plaintiffs' favor would redress that harm. The government argued that any harm to plaintiffs is not fairly traceable to the Secretary's decision because such harm depends on the independent action of third parties choosing to violate their legal duty to respond to the census, and additionally, that the unlawful third-party action would be motivated by unfounded fears that the federal government would itself break the law by using noncitizens' answers against them for law enforcement purposes. The Court rejected the government's argument. Plaintiffs "have met their burden of showing that third parties will react in predictable ways to the citizenship question, even if they do so unlawfully and despite the requirement that the Government keep individual answers confidential. Given the evidence at trial that noncitizen households have historically responded at lower rates than other groups, the plaintiffs' theory of standing "does not rest on mere speculation about the decision of third parties; it relies instead on the predictable effect of Government action on the decisions of third parties."

[The Court (Roberts, C.J., joined by Ginsburg, Breyer, Sotomayor, and Kagan, JJ.) upheld the district court's determination that the Secretary's action in adding the citizenship question was arbitrary and capricious in that it "does not match the explanation the Secretary gave for his decision" and the reasons given were "contrived."].

12–4.3 CONGRESSIONAL STANDING

Unabridged, p. 1507; add to end of *Notes*, new Note 4:

4.   *Arizona State Legislature v. Arizona Independent Redistricting Commission*, 576 U.S. ___, 135 S.Ct. 2652, 192 L.Ed.2d 704 (2015). In 2000, the voters of Arizona approved a ballot initiative to remove all redistricting authority from the state legislature and transfer it to an independent redistricting commission. They sought to prevent partisan gerrymandering of congressional legislative districts. The State legislature sued claiming that the initiative for congressional districting violates the Elections Clause (U.S. Const., Art. I, § 4, cl. 1), which provides that the times, places and manner of congressional elections "shall be prescribed in each State by the *Legislature* thereof" unless Congress alters such laws or regulations. The Arizona legislature argued that it "must have at least the opportunity to engage (or decline to engage) in redistricting before the State may involve other actors in the redistricting process." (The Arizona redistricting commission also drew state legislative districts, but that raises no issue under the Elections Clause.)

Ginsburg, J., for the Court (5 to 4), held, first, the legislature had standing to sue because its claim that the voter proposition stripped it of constitutional authority was a concrete and particularized injury. *Raines v. Byrd* (1997) held that "*six individual Members* of Congress lacked standing to challenge the Line Item Veto Act." In contrast, the Arizona Legislature "is an institutional plaintiff asserting an institutional injury, and it commenced this action after authorizing votes in both of its chambers."

On the merits, the Court held that the Elections Clause does not preclude a voter initiative that creates an alternative way of redistricting. "The dominant purpose" of the Elections Clause "was to empower Congress to override state election rules, not to restrict the way States enact legislation." The Court rejected the argument that the word "legislature" means the representative body that makes the laws of the people. "The exercise of the initiative, we acknowledge, was not at issue in our prior decisions." Nonetheless, "we see no constitutional barrier to a State's empowerment of its people by embracing that form of lawmaking." The Court should not interpret the Elections Clause "to single out federal elections as the one area in which States may not use citizen initiatives as an alternative legislative process."

The Court emphasized the public policy in favor of taking redistricting away from the legislature. While the redistricting commissions have not eliminated partisan suspicions associated with political line-drawing, they limit the conflict of interest when the legislature controls redistricting. They "impede legislators from choosing their voters instead of facilitating the voters' choice of their representatives."

Roberts, C.J., dissented, joined by Scalia, Thomas & Alito, JJ, arguing that the Court's decision has "no basis in the text, structure, or history of the Constitution," which "contains seventeen provisions referring to the 'Legislature' of a 'State,' many of which cannot possibly be read to mean 'the people.'" The 17th Amendment "transferred power to choose United States Senators from 'the Legislature' of each State, Art. I, § 3, to 'the people thereof.' The Amendment resulted from an arduous, decades-long campaign in which reformers across the country worked hard to garner approval from Congress and three-quarters of the States. What chumps! Didn't they realize that all they had to do was interpret the constitutional term 'the Legislature' to mean 'the people'?"

Scalia and Thomas each filed separate dissents, and joined each other's dissents, arguing the legislature lacks standing to assert a claim against another entity of state government. Scalia added that he would normally not express an opinion on the merits, but the majority's resolution is "so utterly devoid of textual or historic support" that he "cannot avoid adding my vote to the devastating dissent of the Chief Justice."

WHERE TO GO FROM HERE

SEEK GOD

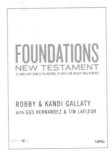

THE PRODIGAL SON
Discovering the Fullness of Life
in the Love of the Father
Matt Carter

Learn what it truly means to be loved and forgiven by
Jesus, and discover the best life is found in the love of
your Father.

Leader Kit $79.99
Bible Study Book $13.99

EXERCISE FAITH

HELP MY UNBELIEF
Why Doubt Is Not the Enemy of Faith
Barnabas Piper

Discover the God who not only desires our belief but
actually welcomes our curiosity.

Leader Kit $79.99
Bible Study Book $13.99

ENGAGE WITH SCRIPTURE

FOUNDATIONS: NEW TESTAMENT
A 260-Day Bible Reading Plan for Busy Believers
Robby and Kandi Gallaty

Study all 27 books of the New Testament in one year
by reading Scripture passages and related devotions
five days each week.

Book $13.99

Prices and availability subject to change without notice.